D1314815

FAMILY STRUCTURE AND SUPPORT ISSUES

FAMILY STRUCTURE AND SUPPORT ISSUES

ANNE E. BENNETT
EDITOR

Nova Science Publishers, Inc.
New York

Copyright © 2007 by Nova Science Publishers, Inc.

NOTICE TO THE READER
The Publisher has taken reasonable care in the preparation of this book, but makes no expressed or implied warranty of any kind and assumes no responsibility for any errors or omissions. No liability is assumed for incidental or consequential damages in connection with or arising out of information contained in this book. The Publisher shall not be liable for any special, consequential, or exemplary damages resulting, in whole or in part, from the readers' use of, or reliance upon, this material.

Independent verification should be sought for any data, advice or recommendations contained in this book. In addition, no responsibility is assumed by the publisher for any injury and/or damage to persons or property arising from any methods, products, instructions, ideas or otherwise contained in this publication.

This publication is designed to provide accurate and authoritative information with regard to the subject matter cover herein. It is sold with the clear understanding that the Publisher is not engaged in rendering legal or any other professional services. If legal, medical or any other expert assistance is required, the services of a competent person should be sought. FROM A DECLARATION OF PARTICIPANTS JOINTLY ADOPTED BY A COMMITTEE OF THE AMERICAN BAR ASSOCIATION AND A COMMITTEE OF PUBLISHERS.

Library of Congress Cataloging-in-Publication Data
Family structure and support issues / Anne E. Bennett (Editor).
    p. cm.
Includes index.
ISBN 13 978-1-60021-340-3
ISBN 10 1-60021-340-5
1. Social legislation--United States. 2. Domestic relations--United States. I. Bennett, Anne E.
KF3300.F29   2006
344.7301--dc22   2006021282

Published by Nova Science Publishers, Inc. ✛New York

CONTENTS

PREFACE

As populations in many developed countries begin to twindle or become heavily unbalanced toward the aged, the support familes, their structures and societal encouragement become vital issues. This book examines some of the perplexing and complex issues involved in this battle for survival.

Chapter 1 - The 109th Congress is considering legislation to extend funding and possibly amend the block grant of Temporary Assistance for Needy Families (TANF), which was created in the 1996 welfare reform law. The original funding authority provided in the 1996 law expired at the end of FY2002. Since then, Congress has inconclusively debated legislation to reauthorize TANF (and some related programs) but has kept the program alive through temporary extensions. The latest such extension is scheduled to expire on September 30, 2005. Reauthorization bills introduced for the 109th Congress (H.R. 240, S. 667) have policies that mirror those of bills considered during the previous three years. This chapter responds to some frequently asked questions about TANF — about its caseload, funding, and how states have complied with work participation rules. It will be updated as new data to respond to these questions become available. Additionally, if new questions are frequently asked, responses to them will also be added to this chapter. This chapter does not provide a description or detailed background information about TANF current law or pending legislation, but refers readers to other Congressional Research Service (CRS) reports for that information.

Chapter 2 - The Temporary Assistance for Needy Families (TANF) block grant provides grants to states to help them fund a wide variety of benefits and services to low-income families with children. TANF is best known as helping fund ongoing cash welfare benefits for families with children, but the block grant may also fund other benefits and services such as emergency payments, child care, transportation assistance, and other social services. Welfare programs are not usually associated with responses to natural disasters. However, the scope of Hurricane Katrina's displacement of families, the strain likely to be placed on human service agencies responding to this displacement, plus the flexibility allowed states to design programs under TANF, has made the block grant a potential source of help to the victims of this disaster. H.R. 3672, which cleared the Congress on September 15, 2005, would provide some additional TANF funds and waive certain program requirements for states affected by Katrina. That same day Senators Grassley and Baucus introduced S. 1716, which would expand upon provisions of H.R. 3672. The TANF block grant is a fixed amount of funding paid to each state based on a formula. States design and administer benefits and services funded by TANF and have wide latitude in their use of block grant funds. States are required to share a portion of the cost of TANF benefits and services by expending some of their own funds on TANF-related benefits and services through a "maintenance of effort" requirement. TANF was created in the 1996 welfare reform law (P.L. 104-193), when it replaced the New Deal program of Aid to Families with Dependent Children (AFDC), which helped states fund cash welfare benefits. The funding authority provided in the 1996 law originally expired at the end of FY2002 (September 30, 2002). Since then, Congress has inconclusively debated legislation to provide for a five-year reauthorization of TANF and instead has enacted temporary extensions of the program. The latest of these extensions is set to expire on September 30, 2005.

Chapter 3 - Medical child support is the legal provision of payment of medical, dental, prescription, and other health care expenses of dependent children. It can include provisions to cover health insurance costs as well as cash payments for unreimbursed medical expenses. According to 2001 Child Support Enforcement (CSE) data, 93% of medical child support is provided in the form of health insurance coverage. The requirement for medical child support is apart of all child support orders (administered by CSE agencies), and it only pertains to the parent's dependent children. Activities undertaken by CSE agencies to establish and enforce medical child support are eligible for federal reimbursement at the CSE matching rate of 66%. The medical child support process requires that a state CSE agency *notify* the employer of a noncustodial parent who owes child support, that the parent is obligated to provide health care coverage for his or her dependent children. CSE agencies notify employers of a medical child support order via a standardized federal form called the National Medical Support Notice. The plan administrator must then determine whether family health care coverage is available for which the dependent children may be eligible. If eligible, the plan administrator is required to enroll the dependent child in an appropriate plan, and notify the noncustodial parent's employer of the premium amount to be withheld from the employee's paycheck. Although establishment of a medical support order is a prerequisite to enforcing the order, inclusion of a health insurance order does not necessarily mean that health insurance coverage is actually provided. According to CSE program data, in 2001, only 49% of child support orders included health insurance coverage, and the health insurance order was complied with in only 18% of the cases. Most policymakers agree that health care coverage for dependent children must be available, accessible, affordable, and stable. Since 1977 and sporadically through 1998, Congress has passed legislation to help states effectively establish and enforce medical child support. The National Medical Support Notice, mandated by 1998 law and promulgated in March 2001, was viewed as a means to significantly improve enforcement of medical child support — to date only about half the states are using the Notice. The 1998 law also called for an advisory body to design a medical child support incentive which would become part of the CSE performance-based incentive payment system — a recommendation was made to Congress in 2001 to indefinitely delay development of a medical child support incentive mainly because it was argued that the appropriate data was not yet available upon which to base such an incentive. Improving the establishment and enforcement of medical child support has been hampered to some extent by factors such as high health care costs, a decline in employer-provided health insurance coverage, an increase in the share of health insurance costs borne by employees, and the large number of uninsured children. This chapter provides a legislative history of medical support provisions in the CSE program, describes current policy with respect to medical child support, examines available data, and discusses some of the issues related to medical child support.

Chapter 4 - The Child Support Enforcement (CSE) program was enacted in 1975 as a federal-state program (Title IV-D of the Social Security Act) to help strengthen families by securing financial support for children from their noncustodial parent on a consistent and continuing basis and by helping some families to remain self-sufficient and off public assistance by providing the requisite CSE services. Over the years, CSE has evolved into a multifaceted program. While cost-recovery still remains an important function of the program, its other aspects include service delivery and promotion of self-sufficiency and parental responsibility. In FY2004, the CSE program collected $21.9 billion in child support payments and served 15.9 million child support cases. However, the program still collects only 18% of child support obligations for which it has responsibility and collects payments for only 51% of its caseload.

Chapter 5 - P.L. 104-193 (the 1996 welfare reform legislation) made major changes to the Child Support Enforcement (CSE) program. Some of the changes include requiring states to increase the percentage of fathers identified, establishing an integrated, automated network linking all states to information about the location and assets of parents, and requiring states to implement more enforcement techniques to obtain collections from debtor parents. Additional legislative changes were made in 1997, 1998, and 1999, but not in 2000, 2001, or 2002. This chapter describes several aspects of the revised CSE program and discusses three issues that probably will be reexamined by the 108th Congress — CSE financing, parental access by noncustodial parents, and distribution of support payments.

Chapter 6 - Among other things, P.L. 109-171 (the budget reconciliation measure, now referred to as the Deficit Reduction Act of 2005 — S. 1932) made a number of changes to the Child Support Enforcement (CSE) program. The act will reduce the federal matching rate for laboratory costs associated with paternity establishment from 90% to 66%, end the federal matching of state expenditures of federal CSE incentive payments reinvested back into the program, and require states to assess a $25 annual user fee for child support services provided to families with no connection to the welfare system. P.L. 109-171 also simplifies CSE distribution rules and extends the "families first" policy by providing incentives to states to encourage them to allow more child support to go to both former welfare families and families still on welfare. In addition, P.L. 109-171 revises some child support enforcement collection mechanisms and adds others. The Congressional Budget Office (CBO) estimates that the CSE provisions contained in P.L. 109-171 will reduce federal costs of the CSE program by $1.5 billion over the five-year period FY2006-FY2010.

Chapter 7 - This chapter provides background on the eligibility and notification requirements for taking leave under the Family and Medical Leave Act ("FMLA"). The FMLA guarantees eligible employees 12 workweeks of unpaid leave for the birth or adoption of a child; for the placement of a foster child; for the care of a spouse, child, or parent suffering from a serious health condition; or for a serious health condition that makes the employee unable to perform the functions of the employee's position. Since the FMLA's enactment in 1993, the U.S. Supreme Court has considered two cases involving the statute. *Ragsdale v. Wolverine World Wide, Inc.* and *Nevada Department of Human Resources v. Hibbs* are discussed in this chapter. The report will be updated in response to the FMLA's amendment and relevant Supreme Court cases. The Family and Medical Leave Act ("FMLA") guarantees eligible employees 12 workweeks of unpaid leave for certain specified reasons.[1] Enacted in 1993, the FMLA seeks "to balance the demands of the workplace with the needs of families, to promote the stability and economic security of families, and to promote national interests in preserving family integrity."[2] This chapter provides background on the eligibility and notification requirements for taking leave under the FMLA, and discusses U.S. Supreme Court cases that have considered the validity of FMLA regulations and the availability of money damages under the FMLA for state employees.

Chapter 8 - This chapter discusses *Ayotte v. Planned Parenthood of Northern New England*, which will be decided by the U.S. Supreme Court this term. The case involves the constitutionality of the New Hampshire Parental Notification Prior to Abortion Act. In November 2004, the U.S. Court of Appeals for the First Circuit invalidated the act because it does not include an explicit exception that would waive the measure's requirements to preserve the health of the pregnant minor. Ayotte, the Attorney General of New Hampshire, contends that a judicial bypass procedure included in the act and other state statutes sufficiently preserve the health of a minor. The Court will review that position, and consider whether the First Circuit applied the correct standard of review when it heard the case in 2004.

Chapter 9 - Massachusetts became the first state to legalize marriage between same-sex couples on May 17, 2004, as a result of a November 2003 decision by the state's highest court that denying gay and lesbian couples the right to marry violated the state's constitution. Currently, federal law does not recognize same-sex marriages. This chapter discusses the Defense of Marriage Act (DOMA), P.L. 104-199, which prohibits federal recognition of same-sex marriages and allows individual states to refuse to recognize such marriages performed in other states, and discusses the potential legal challenges to DOMA. Moreover, this chapter summarizes the legal principles applied in determining the validity of a marriage contracted in another state, surveys the various approaches employed by states to prevent same-sex marriage, and examines the recent House and Senate Resolutions introduced in the 109th Congress proposing a constitutional amendment (H.J.Res. 39, S.J.Res. 1, and S.J.Res. 13) and limiting Federal courts' jurisdiction to hear or determine any question pertaining to the interpretation of DOMA (H.R. 1100).

In: Family Structure and Support Issues   ISBN: 1-60021-340-5
Editor: A. E. Bennett, pp. 1-18   © 2007 Nova Science Publishers, Inc.

Chapter 1

THE TEMPORARY ASSISTANCE FOR NEEDY FAMILIES (TANF) BLOCK GRANT: RESPONSES TO FREQUENTLY ASKED QUESTIONS[*]

Gene Falk

ABSTRACT

The 109th Congress is considering legislation to extend funding and possibly amend the block grant of Temporary Assistance for Needy Families (TANF), which was created in the 1996 welfare reform law. The original funding authority provided in the 1996 law expired at the end of FY2002. Since then, Congress has inconclusively debated legislation to reauthorize TANF (and some related programs) but has kept the program alive through temporary extensions. The latest such extension is scheduled to expire on September 30, 2005. Reauthorization bills introduced for the 109th Congress (H.R. 240, S. 667) have policies that mirror those of bills considered during the previous three years.

This chapter responds to some frequently asked questions about TANF — about its caseload, funding, and how states have complied with work participation rules. It will be updated as new data to respond to these questions become available. Additionally, if new questions are frequently asked, responses to them will also be added to this chapter. This chapter does

---

[*] Excerpted from CRS Report RL32760, dated August 23, 2005.

not provide a description or detailed background information about TANF current law or pending legislation, but refers readers to other Congressional Research Service (CRS) reports for that information.

Caseload

In December of 2004, a total of 2.1 million needy families with children received cash assistance from TANF or from related state programs. The number of families receiving cash assistance is down by more than half (58%) from the historical peak of 5.1 million families receiving cash assistance in March of 1994.

Funding

TANF provides fixed funding to states — the bulk of the funding is provided in a $16.5 billion per year basic block grant. The grant is not adjusted for changes in the cash welfare caseload (see above) or for inflation. From FY1997 through FY2004, the TANF cash grant lost 15% of its value (purchasing power) because of inflation.

In FY2004, states transferred $2.7 billion to other block grants (15.9% of the TANF block grant): $1.9 billion to the child care block grant and $0.8 billion to the Social Services Block Grant. As of September 30, 2004 (end of FY2004), there remained a total of $3.8 billion in unspent TANF funds.

Work Requirements

Though TANF law sets a statutory standard that a state must have 50% of its caseload (that includes an adult or teen parent) participating in work or work activities, this standard is reduced by a "caseload reduction credit." The caseload reduction credit reduces the TANF work participation standard one percentage point for each percent decline in the caseload since FY1995. In FY2003, this meant that 20 states had effective (after credit) standards of 0%. States actually achieved a 31.3% participation rate in FY2003 — well below the 50% statutory standard, but high enough above the effective (after credit) standards so that all states except Nevada and Guam met the 50% participation standard.

This chapter provides responses to frequently asked questions about the Temporary Assistance for Needy Families (TANF) block grant. It is intended as a quick reference to provide easy access to information and data.

CURRENT STATUS OF THE PROGRAM AND LEGISLATION

Why Is Welfare Legislation Being Considered in the 109th Congress?

The original funding authority for TANF, mandatory child care, and state grants for abstinence education provided in the 1996 welfare law expired at the end of FY2002 (September 30, 2002). Since then, Congress has inconclusively debated legislation that would have provided a multiyear reauthorization of the program. These programs have been continued under stop-gap, temporary measures, the latest of which will expire on September 30, 2005. Congress thus faces the issue of welfare reauthorization.

Table 1. Temporary Extensions of Welfare Reform Programs, FY2003-FY2005

Public law	Time period	Notes
P.L. 107-294	Jan. 1, 2003-Mar. 31, 2003	Extension as part of a continuing resolution.
P.L. 108-7	Apr. 1, 2003-June 30, 2003	Extension as a part of the Consolidated Appropriations Act.
P.L. 108-40	July 1, 2003-Sept. 30, 2003	Free-standing bill that amended the Social Security Act to extend TANF and related programs.
P.L. 108-89	Oct. 1, 2003-Mar. 31, 2004	Multipurpose bill that extended programs through the first half of FY2004.
P.L. 108-210	Apr. 1, 2004-June 30, 2004	Free-standing bill extending funding authority for the program through June 30, 2004.
P.L. 108-262	July 1, 2004-Sept. 30, 2004	Free-standing bill extending funding authority for the program through Sept. 30, 2004.
P.L. 108-308	Oct. 1, 2004- Mar. 31, 2005	Free-standing bill to extend funding authority for the programs through Mar. 31, 2005.
P.L. 109-4	Apr. 1, 2005-June 30, 2005	Free-standing bill to extend funding authority for the programs through June 30, 2005.
P.L. 109-19	July 1, 2005-Sept. 30, 2005.	Free-standing bill to extend funding authority for the programs through Sept. 30, 2005.

Source: Congressional Research Service (CRS).

How Many Times Has Congress Enacted Temporary Extensions of TANF?

H.R. 3021, signed by the President July 1, 2005 (P.L. 109-19), was the tenth temporary extension of TANF. Table 1 provides a listing of the laws that have extended TANF, up to the latest extension, which runs until September 30, 2005. These extensions have *not* changed TANF policy, and the program has been operating in FY2003-FY2005 just as it did in FY2002.

Is There an Administration Proposal to Reauthorize TANF?

Yes. In February 2002, the Bush Administration issued its proposal to reauthorize and amend TANF, *Working Toward Independence*.[1]

Has There Been Legislative Action to Reauthorize TANF Since 2002?

The House passed a bill in May 2002 (H.R. 4737, 107th Congress), generally aligned with the President's proposal. An alternative bill was reported from the Senate Finance Committee that July but the full Senate never took up the bill.

Early in the 108th Congress, the House again passed a bill that generally followed the Administration proposal (H.R. 4, 108th Congress, passed the House in February 2003). Eight months later, the Senate Finance Committee again reported a substitute measure. The Finance Committee bill came to the Senate floor in late March 2004, but its consideration was set aside on April 1, 2004 when a motion to limit debate on the bill failed to muster the needed 60 votes. The bill never reappeared on the floor for consideration. Reauthorization bills being considered in the 109th Congress (H.R. 240, S. 667) have policies that mirror those of the bills considered during the previous three years.

THE CASH WELFARE CASELOAD

How Many Families and Recipients Currently Receive Cash Welfare?

In December 2004 (latest data available) about 2.1 million families received cash welfare either funded from TANF block grants or state programs with expenditures countable toward the TANF maintenance of effort requirement. For state-specific caseload numbers, see Appendix A, Table A1.

How Much Has the Cash Welfare Caseload Declined Since the Mid-1990s?

Historically, the cash welfare caseload peaked in March 1994 at 5.1 million families. The 2.1 million families receiving cash welfare as of December 2004 represents a decline of 58% since its historical peak. Figure 1 shows the trend nationally in the number of families receiving cash assistance from October 1975 to December 2004. Table A1 shows state-by-state the number of families receiving cash welfare in December 1994, 2000, 2003, and 2004.

PROGRAM FUNDING

Are There any Adjustments to the TANF Block Grant for Changes in Circumstances?

No. Aside from contingency funds for a recession and bonus funds based on state performance, the amount of funds received by the states is fixed and not adjusted for either inflation or changes in the cash welfare caseload.

How Much Has the TANF Grant Declined in Value Because of Inflation?

From FY1997 (the first year of TANF funding) through FY2004 (ended September 30, 2004), the real value of the basic TANF block grant declined by 15%. Based on inflation projected by the Congressional Budget Office (CBO) in

August 2005, the block grant would decline by 26% from FY1997 through FY2010. Table 2 shows the value of the basic TANF block grant from FY1997 through FY2010 in constant 1997 dollars.

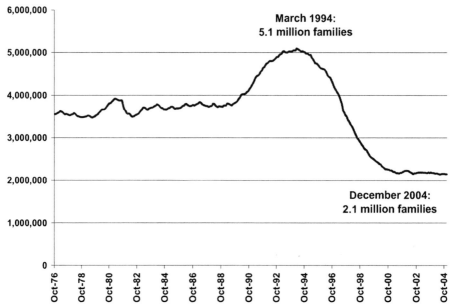

Source: Congressional Research Service (CRS) based on data from the U.S. Department of Health and Human Services (HHS).

Figure 1. Number of Needy Families with Children Receiving Cash Welfare: October 1976-December 2004

How Much of the TANF Grant Has Been Transferred to the Child Care and Social Service Block Grants?

In FY2004 (the latest year for which data are available) states transferred a total of $2.7 billion (15.9% of the block grant): $1.9 billion (11.2% of the TANF block grant) to the child care block grant and $0.8 billion (4.7% of the block grant) to the Social Services Block Grant (SSBG). See Table A2 for transfers by state.

Cumulatively over the lifetime of TANF (FY1997-FY2004), a total of $21.0 billion (15.9% of the block grant) has been transferred: $13.5 billion (10.2% of the TANF block grant) to the child care block grant and $7.5 billion (5.7% of the

TANF block grant) to SSBG. Table A3 shows cumulative transfers by state to the child care block grant and SSBG.

Table 2. Basic TANF Block Grant in Constant 1997 Dollars

Fiscal Year	Value of the Block Grant in Bilions of FY1997 Dollars	Cumulative Loss of Value (in percent)
1997	$16.5	
1998	16.2	-2%
1999	15.9	-3%
2000	15.4	-6%
2001	14.9	-9%
2002	14.7	-11%
2003	14.4	-13%
2004	14.1	-15%
2005	13.6	-17%
2006	13.3	-20%
2007	13.0	-21%
2008	12.7	-23%
2009	12.4	-25%
2010	12.2	-26%

Source: Table prepared by the Congressional Research Service (CRS). Constant dollars were computed using the Consumer Price Index for all Urban Consumers (CPI-U). Actual inflation was used to compute constant dollars for FY1997-FY2004 using data from the U.S. Bureau of Labor Statistics. Constant dollars for FY2005 through FY2010 are based on the inflation assumptions of the Congressional Budget Office (CBO), published in August. 2005.

How Much of the TANF Grant Has Gone Unspent?

At the end of FY2004 (September 30, 2004, the latest data available), a total of $3.8 billion of TANF block grants had not either been transferred or spent. This represents 2.8% of all TANF grants provided to the states over the FY1997-FY2004 period.

Some of the $3.8 billion in unspent TANF funds represents funds for commitments that states already made. Through the end of September 2004, states had made commitments to spend — obligations — that have yet to result in expenditures totaling $1.9 billion. Generally, obligations are binding commitments to spend in the form of contracts, grants, or other types of commitments to provide benefits and services. However, the definition of "obligation" varies from program to program, and since TANF essentially comprises 54 different programs, what constitutes an obligation may vary among the states.

The remaining $1.9 billion in unspent funds is called the "unobligated balance." These are the funds states have available for new commitments.

Table A4 shows TANF unspent funds available as of September 30, 2003 by state. Note that some transfers from TANF may remain unspent in the child care block grant and SSBG program; such unspent transfers are *not* included in the figures for unspent TANF funds.

TANF WORK PARTICIPATION STANDARDS

What is the TANF Work Participation Standard States Must Meet?

The TANF statute requires states to have 50% of their caseload with an adult or teen household head meet standards of participation in work or activities — that is, a family member must be in specified activities for a minimum number of hours. There is a separate participation standard that applies to the two-parent portion of a state's caseload, requiring 90% of its two-parent caseload to meet participation standards.

However, the statutory work participation standards are reduced by a "caseload reduction credit," which reduces TANF work participation standards one percentage point for each percent decline in a state's cash welfare caseload from FY1995. This has significantly reduced the effective (after credit) work participation standard states must meet. For FY2003 work participation (latest data currently available), the caseload reduction credit reduced participation standards to 0% in 20 states. (That is, the caseload reduction credit equaled or exceeded 50%.)

Table A5 shows the statutory and effective (after-credit) work participation standards and actual work participation rates achieved by states for FY2003 for all families. Table A6 shows the same information for the two-parent portion of the caseload.

What Actual Work Participation Rates Have the States Achieved?

In FY2003 (latest year of available data), the national average work participation rate for all families achieved by states was 31.3% — well below the statutory 50% participation standard, but, because of the caseload reduction credit, high enough so that all jurisdictions except Nevada and Guam met the FY2003 standard. The participation rate achieved nationwide for the two-parent portion of the caseload was 48.4%. In FY2003, Arkansas, the District of Columbia, Guam, and West Virginia failed to meet the two-parent standard.

Actual work participation rates for each state are shown on Table A5 (all family rates) and Table A6 (two-parent family rates).

APPENDIX: STATE TABLES

Table A1. Number of Families Receiving Cash Assistance: December 1994, 2000, 2003, and 2004

State	Dec-94	Dec-00	Dec-03	Dec-04	Percentage Change to Dec 04 from Dec-94	Dec-00	Dec-03
Alabama	47,903	18,959	19,745	21,119	-55.9	11.4	7.0
Alaska	12,370	5,586	4,900	4,577	-63.0	-18.1	-6.6
Arizona	72,158	32,156	52,170	45,917	-36.4	42.8	-12.0
Arkansas	25,047	11,132	10,695	8,771	-65.0	-21.2	-18.0
California	923,358	529,918	493,139	511,175	-44.6	-3.5	3.7
Colorado	40,244	10,623	14,654	15,076	-62.5	41.9	2.9
Connecticut	60,965	27,694	24,939	24,265	-60.2	-12.4	-2.7
Delaware	11,227	5,543	5,830	5,866	-47.8	5.8	0.6
District of Columbia	27,420	16,675	17,617	17,727	-35.4	6.3	0.6
Florida	238,682	65,111	61,413	66,974	-71.9	2.9	9.1
Georgia	141,154	51,393	58,004	46,336	-67.2	-9.8	-20.1
Hawaii	21,489	19,243	12,543	11,574	-46.1	-39.9	-7.7
Idaho	8,953	1,309	1,844	1,887	-78.9	44.2	2.3
Illinois	241,091	69,941	35,401	39,488	-83.6	-43.5	11.5
Indiana	69,933	40,683	54,983	52,010	-25.6	27.8	-5.4
Iowa	38,022	20,436	21,589	21,494	-43.5	5.2	-0.4
Kansas	28,838	12,567	16,156	17,441	-39.5	38.8	8.0
Kentucky	76,824	36,754	35,728	35,569	-53.7	-3.2	-0.4
Louisiana	82,792	26,435	21,215	17,184	-79.2	-35.0	-19.0
Maine	22,025	11,417	10,982	11,676	-47.0	2.3	6.3
Maryland	80,890	30,660	29,776	27,864	-65.6	-9.1	-6.4
Massachusetts	105,769	42,829	50,420	49,586	-53.1	15.8	-1.7
Michigan	209,695	69,055	79,051	81,007	-61.4	17.3	2.5
Minnesota	61,343	37,830	39,213	32,657	-46.8	-13.7	-16.7
Mississippi	53,221	15,825	19,769	17,272	-67.5	9.1	-12.6
Missouri	91,802	50,788	48,586	47,807	-47.9	-5.9	-1.6
Montana	11,660	4,697	5,349	4,743	-59.3	1.0	-11.3
Nebraska	15,013	9,941	12,170	11,930	-20.5	20.0	-2.0

Table A1. Continued

State	Dec-94	Dec-00	Dec-03	Dec-04	Percentage Change to Dec 04 from Dec-94	Dec-00	Dec-03
Nevada	15,559	6,932	9,995	8,339	-46.4	20.3	-16.6
New Hampshire	11,078	5,586	6,113	6,232	-43.7	11.6	1.9
New Jersey	120,908	48,284	45,363	48,416	-60.0	0.3	6.7
New Mexico	34,854	21,856	17,606	18,083	-48.1	-17.3	2.7
New York	463,692	234,866	195,972	194,689	-58.0	-17.1	-0.7
North Carolina	128,848	45,199	39,124	36,466	-71.7	-19.3	-6.8
North Dakota	5,309	2,886	3,190	2,873	-45.9	-0.5	-9.9
Ohio	236,298	86,563	84,781	84,937	-64.1	-1.9	0.2
Oklahoma	45,893	14,548	14,921	13,691	-70.2	-5.9	-8.2
Oregon	39,967	16,033	18,223	19,836	-50.4	23.7	8.9
Pennsylvania	208,949	84,175	85,198	96,642	-53.7	14.8	13.4
Puerto Rico	56,132	26,956	18,211	15,544	-72.3	-42.3	-14.6
Rhode Island	22,599	16,725	14,533	13,620	-39.7	-18.6	-6.3
South Carolina	50,251	18,110	19,973	18,629	-62.9	2.9	-6.7
South Dakota	6,521	2,750	2,809	2,842	-56.4	3.3	1.2
Tennessee	105,616	58,585	73,538	73,236	-30.7	25.0	-0.4
Texas	281,011	133,685	118,536	98,721	-64.9	-26.2	-16.7
Utah	17,240	7,641	9,081	4,730	-72.6	-38.1	-47.9
Vermont	9,707	5,577	5,183	5,088	-47.6	-8.8	-1.8
Virginia	74,203	30,479	35,077	37,725	-49.2	23.8	7.5
Washington	102,603	57,077	56,640	58,719	-42.8	2.9	3.7
West Virginia	39,546	14,129	16,340	13,607	-65.6	-3.7	-16.7
Wisconsin	73,714	17,915	22,400	21,748	-70.5	21.4	-2.9
Wyoming	5,400	569	382	336	-93.8	-40.9	-12.0
Guam	2,088	2,554	3,072	3,072	47.1	20.3	0.0
Virgin Islands	1,264	771	539	504	-60.1	-34.6	-6.5
Totals	4,979,138	2,235,651	2,174,681	2,147,317	-56.9	-4.0	-1.3

Source: Congressional Research Service (CRS) based on data from the U.S. Department of Health and Human Services (HHS).

Table A2. TANF Transfers to the Child Care and Social Services Block Grant, FY2004 ($ in millions)

State	Transfers to CCDBG		Transfers to SSBG		Total transfers	
	Dollars	Percent of total grants	Dollars	Percent of total grants	Dollars	Percent of total grants
Alabama	19.9	18.7	10.6	10.0	30.6	28.7
Alaska	15.4	24.2	3.5	5.5	18.9	29.8
Arizona	0.0	0.0	22.6	9.8	22.6	9.8
Arkansas	16.2	24.6	2.7	4.1	18.9	28.7
California	305.2	8.3	87.2	2.4	392.4	10.6
Colorado	28.1	18.8	15.0	10.0	43.1	28.8
Connecticut	0.0	0.0	26.7	10.0	26.7	10.0
Delaware	3.2	9.8	3.3	10.0	6.5	19.8
District of Columbia	18.5	15.7	3.9	3.3	22.4	19.0
Florida	122.5	19.4	62.3	9.8	184.8	29.2
Georgia	29.7	8.1	19.7	5.4	49.4	13.4
Hawaii	7.8	7.9	9.8	10.0	17.6	17.9
Idaho	6.8	19.1	3.6	10.0	10.3	29.1
Illinois	0.0	0.0	34.0	5.8	34.0	5.8
Indiana	4.1	1.9	2.0	0.9	6.1	2.8
Iowa	27.6	20.3	11.9	8.8	39.5	29.0
Kansas	21.5	21.2	4.3	4.3	25.8	25.5
Kentucky	46.3	25.1	0.0	0.0	46.3	25.1
Louisiana	22.1	12.3	16.3	9.1	38.4	21.3
Maine	7.7	9.6	6.9	8.6	14.6	18.1
Maryland	20.3	8.0	22.9	9.0	43.2	17.0
Massachusetts	91.9	19.7	45.9	9.8	137.8	29.5
Michigan	0.0	0.0	26.9	3.4	26.9	3.4
Minnesota	25.0	8.9	4.8	1.7	29.8	10.6
Mississippi	2.8	2.9	9.8	10.0	12.7	12.9
Missouri	25.0	11.0	21.7	9.5	46.7	20.5
Montana	2.0	4.3	2.0	4.3	4.0	8.7
Nebraska	9.0	14.8	0.0	0.0	9.0	14.8
Nevada	0.0	0.0	0.7	1.4	0.7	1.4
New Hampshire	0.1	0.2	0.0	0.0	0.1	0.2
New Jersey	51.2	12.3	15.5	3.7	66.7	16.0
New Mexico	33.0	28.4	2.0	1.7	35.0	30.2
New York	408.0	16.5	122.0	4.9	530.0	21.5
North Carolina	83.8	24.8	6.4	1.9	90.2	26.7
North Dakota	0.0	0.0	0.0	0.0	0.0	0.0

Table A2. Continued

State	Transfers to CCDBG		Transfers to SSBG		Total transfers	
	Dollars	Percent of total grants	Dollars	Percent of total grants	Dollars	Percent of total grants
Ohio	0.0	0.0	75.6	10.0	75.6	10.0
Oklahoma	29.5	19.6	14.8	9.8	44.3	29.4
Oregon	0.0	0.0	0.0	0.0	0.0	0.0
Pennsylvania	165.9	22.9	0.0	0.0	165.9	22.9
Rhode Island	13.1	13.9	0.4	0.4	13.5	14.3
South Carolina	1.3	1.3	10.0	9.6	11.3	10.9
South Dakota	0.0	0.0	2.2	10.0	2.2	10.0
Tennessee	54.1	24.3	0.0	0.0	54.1	24.3
Texas	0.0	0.0	0.0	0.0	0.0	0.0
Utah	0.0	0.0	5.3	6.0	5.3	6.0
Vermont	9.2	18.8	4.7	9.6	14.0	28.4
Virginia	16.8	10.1	15.8	9.5	32.6	19.6
Washington	95.5	24.5	10.7	2.7	106.2	27.3
West Virginia	0.0	0.0	11.4	10.0	11.4	10.0
Wisconsin	65.2	20.0	13.4	4.1	78.6	24.1
Wyoming	0.0	0.0	1.9	9.5	1.9	9.5
Total	1905.3	11.2	793.1	4.7	2698.4	15.9

Source: Table prepared by the Congressional Research Service (CRS) based on data from the U.S. Department of Health and Human Services (HHS).

Table A3. Cumulative TANF Transfers to the Child Care and Social Services Block Grants, FY1997-FY2003 ($ in millions)

State	Transfers to CCDBG		Transfers to SSBG		Total transfers	
	Dollars	Percent of total grants	Dollars	Percent of total grants	Dollars	Percent of total grants
Alabama	165.1	18.6	88.7	10.0	253.8	28.6
Alaska	102.9	22.1	32.1	6.9	135.0	29.0
Arizona	103.6	5.6	174.4	9.4	278.0	15.0
Arkansas	33.2	7.2	11.4	2.5	44.6	9.6
California	2430.8	8.3	442.2	1.5	2873	9.8
Colorado	179.6	16.2	97.4	8.8	276.9	25.0
Connecticut	0.0	0.0	185.0	8.5	185.0	8.5
Delaware	9.6	3.8	13.6	5.4	23.2	9.3
District of Columbia	122.1	14.3	34.2	4.0	156.4	18.3

Table A3. Continued

State	Transfers to CCDBG		Transfers to SSBG		Total transfers	
	Dollars	Percent of total grants	Dollars	Percent of total grants	Dollars	Percent of total grants
Florida	782.7	16.0	446.2	9.1	1228.9	25.1
Georgia	204.3	7.3	181.1	6.5	385.4	13.8
Hawaii	52.8	7.2	28.9	4.0	81.7	11.2
Idaho	46.3	18.3	18.5	7.3	64.8	25.6
Illinois	272.4	6.3	338.2	7.8	610.6	14.1
Indiana	292.2	17.1	74.3	4.4	366.4	21.5
Iowa	152.7	14.7	83.5	8.0	236.2	22.7
Kansas	88.8	10.8	69.6	8.4	158.4	19.2
Kentucky	281.7	19.2	64.7	4.4	346.4	23.7
Louisiana	312.0	22.5	49.1	3.5	361.1	26.0
Maine	60.6	9.7	40.0	6.4	100.6	16.1
Maryland	182.5	9.9	160.4	8.7	342.9	18.6
Massachusetts	751.3	20.2	349.5	9.4	1100.8	29.6
Michigan	296.5	4.7	401.7	6.4	698.2	11.0
Minnesota	164.3	8.1	126.2	6.3	290.5	14.4
Mississippi	103.3	13.8	64.6	8.6	167.9	22.4
Missouri	147.7	8.4	139.5	7.9	287.2	16.3
Montana	52.4	14.7	22.2	6.2	74.6	20.9
Nebraska	45.0	9.7	4.4	0.9	49.4	10.6
Nevada	0.0	0.0	7.0	1.9	7.0	1.9
New Hampshire	1.3	0.4	2.9	0.9	4.3	1.3
New Jersey	364.5	11.6	262.8	8.3	627.3	19.9
New Mexico	170.0	17.9	6.0	0.6	176.0	18.5
New York	1978.8	10.3	1731.4	9.0	3710.2	19.2
North Carolina	464.6	18.1	55.5	2.2	520.1	20.3
North Dakota	0.5	0.3	0.0	0.0	0.5	0.3
Ohio	359.7	6.1	587.3	10.0	947.0	16.1
Oklahoma	239.1	19.9	119.5	10.0	358.6	29.9
Oregon	0.0	0.0	0.0	0.0	0.0	0.0
Pennsylvania	541.5	9.8	196.4	3.5	737.9	13.3
Rhode Island	40.4	5.6	6.9	1.0	47.3	6.6
South Carolina	14.1	1.8	64.6	8.1	78.8	9.8
South Dakota	13.9	8.2	17.1	10.0	31.0	18.2
Tennessee	356.4	21.1	15.6	0.9	372.0	22.1
Texas	164.3	3.9	200.1	4.7	364.4	8.6
Utah	3.7	0.6	37.2	5.5	41.0	6.1
Vermont	58.0	15.1	37.0	9.6	95.0	24.7
Virginia	154.5	12.3	118.3	9.4	272.8	21.7
Washington	646.9	20.8	89.7	2.9	736.6	23.7
West Virginia	15.4	1.8	51.0	5.8	66.4	7.6
Wisconsin	433.6	16.8	176.7	6.8	610.3	23.6
Wyoming	15.5	8.6	17.9	9.9	33.3	18.5
Total	13,473.2	10.2	7,542.6	5.7	21,015.8	15.9

Source: Table prepared by the Congressional Research Service (CRS) based on data from the U.S. Department of Health and Human Services (HHS).

Table A4. Unspent TANF Funds as of September 30, 2004 ($ in millions)

State	Obligated but unspent	Unobligated and unspent	Total unspent funds
Alabama	9.7	22.7	32.4
Alaska	9.3	11.6	20.9
Arizona	25.1	0.0	25.1
Arkansas	0.1	86.0	86.0
California	249.1	0.0	249.1
Colorado	66.2	0.0	66.2
Connecticut	0.0	0.0	0.0
Delaware	1.2	3.9	5.1
District of Columbia	1.5	46.9	48.4
Florida	99.3	0.0	99.3
Georgia	17.9	160.8	178.7
Hawaii	10.9	113.5	124.4
Idaho	9.8	0.0	9.8
Illinois	0.0	0.0	0.0
Indiana	43.8	0.0	43.8
Iowa	5.7	20.4	26.2
Kansas	0.0	5.2	5.2
Kentucky	3.9	62.3	66.2
Louisiana	16.8	0.0	16.8
Maine	0.0	27.6	27.6
Maryland	7.1	66.5	73.6
Massachusetts	1.5	5.1	6.6
Michigan	0.0	111.4	111.4
Minnesota	0.0	69.6	69.6
Mississippi	6.5	1.8	8.3
Missouri	30.7	0.0	30.7
Montana	1.0	20.7	21.8
Nebraska	7.5	0.0	7.5
Nevada	1.2	15.3	16.5
New Hampshire	0.0	47.6	47.6
New Jersey	86.0	94.1	180.2
New Mexico	16.7	13.9	30.6
New York	193.8	239.7	433.6
North Carolina	62.6	0.0	62.6
North Dakota	0.0	12.4	12.4
Ohio	484.8	336.2	821
Oklahoma	74.4	18.1	92.5
Oregon	46.1	0.0	46.1
Pennsylvania	64.0	142.1	206.1
Rhode Island	0.0	0.0	0.0
South Carolina	0.0	1.5	1.5
South Dakota	0.7	22.2	22.9
Tennessee	4.7	16.0	20.7

Table A4. Continued

State	Obligated but unspent	Unobligated and unspent	Total unspent funds
Texas	176.8	2.7	179.5
Utah	0.0	17.5	17.5
Vermont	0.0	0.0	0.0
Virginia	14.0	0.0	14.0
Washington	0.0	3.5	3.5
West Virginia	0.0	3.8	3.8
Wisconsin	0.1	22.5	22.6
Wyoming	13.0	41.1	54.1
Total	1863.5	1886.5	3750

Source: Table prepared by the Congressional Research Service (CRS) based on data from the U.S. Department of Health and Human Services (HHS).

Table A5. TANF Work Participation Standards and Rates for All Families, FY2003, by State

State	Statutory participation standard	Caseload reduction credit	Effective (after credit) standard)	Actual participation rate	State met standard?
Alabama	50.0	-60.4	0.0	37.1	Yes
Alaska	50.0	-38.9	11.1	41.1	Yes
Arizona	50.0	-36.9	13.1	13.4	Yes
Arkansas	50.0	-46.7	3.3	22.4	Yes
California	50.0	-44.2	5.8	24.0	Yes
Colorado	50.0	-67.3	0.0	32.5	Yes
Connecticut	50.0	-29.7	20.3	30.6	Yes
Delaware	50.0	-39.8	10.2	18.2	Yes
Dist. of Col.	50.0	-38.5	11.5	23.1	Yes
Florida	50.0	-70.6	0.0	33.1	Yes
Georgia	50.0	-51.9	0.0	10.9	Yes
Guam	50.0	0.0	50.0	0.0	No
Hawaii	50.0	-30	20.0	65.8	Yes
Idaho	50.0	-30.0	20.0	43.7	Yes
Illinois	50.0	-79.1	0.0	57.8	Yes
Indiana	50.0	-21.1	28.9	40.3	Yes
Iowa	50.0	-42.7	7.3	45.1	Yes
Kansas	50.0	-8.3	41.7	87.9	Yes
Kentucky	50.0	-45.5	4.5	32.8	Yes
Louisiana	50.0	-59.0	0.0	34.6	Yes
Maine	50.0	-47.5	2.5	27.7	Yes
Maryland	50.0	-43.5	6.5	9.1	Yes
Massachusetts	50.0	-45.1	4.9	61.0	Yes
Michigan	50.0	-62.0	0.0	25.3	Yes
Minnesota	50.0	-35.2	14.8	25.0	Yes

Table A5. Continued

State	Statutory participation standard	Caseload reduction credit	Effective (after credit) standard)	Actual participation rate	State met standard?
Mississippi	50.0	-37.4	12.6	17.2	Yes
Missouri	50.0	-45.0	5.0	28.0	Yes
Montana	50.0	-48.0	2.0	85.9	Yes
Nebraska	50.0	-25.8	24.2	33.4	Yes
Nevada	50.0	-23.8	26.2	22.3	No
New Hampshire	50.0	-43.9	6.1	28.2	Yes
New Jersey	50.0	-58.2	0.0	35.0	Yes
New Mexico	50.0	-41.6	8.4	42.0	Yes
New York	50.0	-60.1	0.0	37.1	Yes
North Carolina	50.0	-52.6	0.0	25.3	Yes
North Dakota	50.0	-38	12.0	27.0	Yes
Ohio	50.0	-57.2	0.0	62.3	Yes
Oklahoma	50.0	-53.2	0.0	29.2	Yes
Oregon	50.0	-54.0	0.0	60.0	Yes
Pennsylvania	50.0	-60.6	0.0	9.9	Yes
Puerto Rico	50.0	-46.9	3.1	6.1	Yes
Rhode Island	50.0	-30.8	19.2	24.3	Yes
South Carolina	50.0	-47.6	2.4	54.3	Yes
South Dakota	50.0	-37.6	12.4	46.1	Yes
Tennessee	50.0	-38.4	11.6	42.7	Yes
Texas	50.0	-50.3	0.0	28.1	Yes
Utah	50.0	-33.0	17.0	28.1	Yes
Vermont	50.0	-42.9	7.1	24.3	Yes
Virgin Islands	50.0	-50.2	0.0	5.0	Yes
Virginia	50.0	-56.8	0.0	44.6	Yes
Washington	50.0	-41.8	8.2	46.2	Yes
West Virginia	50.0	-58.7	0.0	14.2	Yes
Wisconsin	50.0	-51.9	0.0	67.2	Yes
Wyoming	50.0	-87.0	0.0	83.0	Yes

Source: Table prepared by the Congressional Research Service (CRS) based on data from the U.S. Department of Health and Human Services (HHS).

Table A6. TANF Work Participation Standards and Rates for Two-Parent Families, FY2003, by State

State	Statutory participation standard	Caseload reduction credit	Effective (after credit) standard)	Actual participation rate	State met standard?
Alabama	90.0	NA	NA	NA	NA
Alaska	90.0	48.8	41.2	44.6	Yes
Arizona	90.0	36.9	53.1	55.3	Yes
Arkansas	90.0	46.7	43.3	31.8	No
California	90.0	NA	NA	NA	NA
Colorado	90.0	67.3	22.7	40.1	Yes
Connecticut	90.0	NA	NA	NA	NA
Delaware	90.0	NA	NA	NA	NA
Dist. of Col.	90.0	49.0	41.0	19.6	No
Florida	90.0	NA	NA	NA	NA
Georgia	90.0	NA	NA	NA	NA
Guam	90.0	0.0	90.0	0.0	No
Hawaii	90.0	NA	NA	NA	NA
Idaho	90.0	80.4	9.6	42.3	Yes
Illinois	90.0	NA	NA	NA	NA
Indiana	90.0	NA	NA	NA	NA
Iowa	90.0	61.1	28.9	39.2	Yes
Kansas	90.0	8.3	81.7	87.1	Yes
Kentucky	90.0	81.0	9.0	46.2	Yes
Louisiana	90.0	59.0	31.0	39.0	Yes
Maine	90.0	79.9	10.1	29.2	Yes
Maryland	90.0	NA	NA	NA	NA
Massachusetts	90.0	45.1	44.9	73.9	Yes
Michigan	90.0	83.6	6.4	36.2	Yes
Minnesota	90.0	NA	NA	NA	NA
Mississippi	90.0	NA	NA	NA	NA
Missouri	90.0	NA	NA	NA	NA
Montana	90.0	48	42.0	95.7	Yes
Nebraska	90.0	NA	NA	NA	NA
Nevada	90.0	NA	NA	NA	NA
New Hampshire	90.0	NA	NA	NA	NA
New Jersey	90.0	NA	NA	NA	NA
New Mexico	90.0	41.6	48.4	52.0	Yes
New York	90.0	79.3	10.7	52.2	Yes
North Carolina	90.0	52.6	37.4	49.2	Yes
North Dakota	90.0	NA	NA	NA	NA
Ohio	90.0	80.3	9.7	67.8	Yes
Oklahoma	90.0	53.2	36.8	50.5	Yes
Oregon	90.0	54.0	36.0	52.7	Yes
Pennsylvania	90.0	83.5	6.5	8.8	Yes
Puerto Rico	90.0	NA	NA	NA	NA
Rhode Island	90.0	30.8	59.2	94.9	Yes

Table A6. Continued

State	Statutory participation standard	Caseload reduction credit	Effective (after credit) standard)	Actual participation rate	State met standard?
South Carolina	90.0	47.6	42.4	50.6	Yes
South Dakota	90.0	NA	NA	NA	NA
Tennessee	90.0	NA	NA	NA	NA
Texas	90.0	NA	NA	NA	NA
Utah	90.0	NA	NA	NA	NA
Vermont	90.0	54.3	35.7	37.5	Yes
Virgin Islands	90.0	NA	NA	NA	NA
Virginia	90.0	NA	NA	NA	NA
Washington	90.0	48.4	41.6	44.3	Yes
West Virginia	90.0	58.7	31.3	25.2	No
Wisconsin	90.0	68.7	21.3	40.3	Yes
Wyoming	90.0	87.0	3.0	91.5	Yes

Sourc e: Table prepared by the Congressional Research Service (CRS) based on data from the U.S. Department of Health and Human Services (HHS).

REFERENCES

[1]   Available   online   from   the   White   House   website   at [http://www.whitehouse.gov/news/releases/2002/02/welfare-reform-announ cement-book.pdf].

In: Family Structure and Support Issues   ISBN: 1-60021-340-5
Editor: A. E. Bennett, pp. 19-25   © 2007 Nova Science Publishers, Inc.

Chapter 2

TEMPORARY ASSISTANCE FOR NEEDY FAMILIES (TANF): ITS ROLE IN RESPONSE TO THE EFFECTS OF HURRICANE KATRINA*

Gene Falk

ABSTRACT

The Temporary Assistance for Needy Families (TANF) block grant provides grants to states to help them fund a wide variety of benefits and services to low-income families with children. TANF is best known as helping fund ongoing cash welfare benefits for families with children, but the block grant may also fund other benefits and services such as emergency payments, child care, transportation assistance, and other social services. Welfare programs are not usually associated with responses to natural disasters. However, the scope of Hurricane Katrina's displacement of families, the strain likely to be placed on human service agencies responding to this displacement, plus the flexibility allowed states to design programs under TANF, has made the block grant a potential source of help to the victims of this disaster. H.R. 3672, which cleared the Congress on September 15, 2005, would provide some additional TANF funds and waive certain program requirements for states affected by Katrina. That same day Senators Grassley and Baucus introduced S. 1716, which would expand upon provisions of H.R. 3672.

---

* Excerpted from CRS Report RS22246, dated September 16, 2005.

The TANF block grant is a fixed amount of funding paid to each state based on a formula. States design and administer benefits and services funded by TANF and have wide latitude in their use of block grant funds. States are required to share a portion of the cost of TANF benefits and services by expending some of their own funds on TANF-related benefits and services through a "maintenance of effort" requirement.[1]

TANF was created in the 1996 welfare reform law (P.L. 104-193), when it replaced the New Deal program of Aid to Families with Dependent Children (AFDC), which helped states fund cash welfare benefits. The funding authority provided in the 1996 law originally expired at the end of FY2002 (September 30, 2002). Since then, Congress has inconclusively debated legislation to provide for a five-year reauthorization of TANF and instead has enacted temporary extensions of the program. The latest of these extensions is set to expire on September 30, 2005.

TANF CASH WELFARE BENEFIT PROGRAMS

TANF is the major federal-state program providing cash assistance to needy families with children. While federal TANF grants help fund this cash assistance, states determine eligibility rules and benefit amounts which vary greatly among the states. There are no federal rules regarding eligibility and benefits for ongoing cash welfare, other than the requirement that it be paid to families with children that meet a financial test of economic need.

Table 1 provides some basic information on cash welfare benefits in the states affected by Hurricane Katrina and some of their neighboring states. It shows both the maximum monthly benefit amount paid to a family of three as of January 2005 and the average number of families that received cash assistance in December 2004. The maximum monthly benefit is generally the amount paid to a family with no other income sources. TANF cash assistance benefits in this region are relatively low compared with those paid in other regions and states. For example, the comparable maximum cash welfare grant paid in New York City in January 2005 was $691 per month and the maximum cash welfare grant paid to a family of three in the urban areas of California was $723 per month.

TANF imposes some requirements on states with respect to families receiving cash assistance. The purpose of the requirements is to ensure that receipt of cash welfare is temporary and to encourage movement off the rolls and into work. TANF requires that a specified percentage of its caseload be engaged in work or job preparation activities, limits federally-funded assistance to five years, and requires that cash assistance recipients cooperate with child support enforcement rules (establish paternity and assign child support to the state).

**Table 1. TANF Cash Welfare Benefits and the Cash Welfare Caseload in
Selected States Affected by Hurricane Katrina**

State	Maximum Monthly Cash Welfare Grant for a Family of 3: January 2005 (unless otherwise noted)	Average Monthly Number of Families Receiving Cash Assistance: December 2004
States directly affected by Hurricane Katrina		
Alabama	$215	21,119
Florida	303	66,974
Louisiana	240	17,184
Mississippi	170	17,272
Selected Neighboring States		
Texas	223	98,721
Arkansas	204 (as of 1/1/04)	8,771
Georgia	280	46,336
Tennessee	185	73,236

Source: TANF cash assistance maximum benefit amounts are based on a Congressional
Research Service (CRS) survey of the states. Cash assistance caseloads are based on
data from the U.S. Department of Health and Human Services (HHS).

EMERGENCY ASSISTANCE

TANF also gives authority to states to pay "emergency assistance" benefits.
Emergency benefits are those that:

- are considered "nonrecurrent, short-term benefits;"
- are designed to deal with a specific crisis situation or episode of need;
- are not intended to meet recurrent or ongoing needs; and
- will not extend beyond four months.[2]

Families receiving such emergency benefits are *not* subject to the same
requirements (i.e, work requirements and time limits) as are families that receive
cash assistance. As with cash welfare, states determine eligibility for and the
scope of emergency benefits provided to low-income families with children.

OTHER BENEFITS AND SERVICES

In addition to ongoing cash welfare and emergency aid, TANF can fund a wide range of other social services for low-income families with children, such as child care, transportation aid, family preservation and support services, and similar types of services. As with ongoing cash welfare and emergency assistance, states determine eligibility and the scope of benefits provided to needy families with children.

LEGISLATION TO RESPOND TO THE IMPACT OF HURRICANE KATRINA

Welfare programs are not usually associated with responses to natural disasters. However, the scope of Hurricane Katrina's displacement of families, the strain likely to be placed on human service agencies responding to this displacement, plus the flexibility allowed states to design programs under TANF, has made the block grant a potential source of help to the victims of this disaster. While TANF funding is flexible and provides states with options to help needy families, there are challenges to the program to help meet emerging needs. First, TANF is a state-based program, with each state operating its own program under its own rules for its own residents. For example, how will Texas provide benefits and services to displaced residents of Louisiana? Second, TANF block grants are fixed amounts determined by formula in federal law. In the above example, if a state such as Texas provides benefits and services to families from Louisiana, they would have to be paid for out of Texas' allocation of TANF funds. Third, in terms of ongoing cash assistance, there are questions about applying some of the 1996 welfare reforms (work requirements and time limits) to victims of a natural disaster.

H.R. 3672, which passed the House on September 8, 2005 and the Senate on September 15, 2005 would address some of these issues by:

- Providing extra funding for three states directly impacted by Hurricane Katrina — Alabama, Louisiana, and Mississippi.
- Federalizing the costs of benefits paid by a host state to evacuees from states directly impacted by Hurricane Katrina for one year. The measures would provide 100% federal funding for such benefits, though limited to 20% of a state's basic block grant in the year.

Table 2. Comparison of House and Senate Versions of H.R. 3672

Provision	H.R. 3672 (as passed both the House and Senate)	TANF Provisions of S. 1716
Additional funding for states directly impacted by Hurricane Katrina	Permits Alabama, Louisiana, and Mississippi to draw up to 20% of their block grant from the TANF loan fund, with the loan and its interest forgiven.	Permits Alabama, Louisiana, and Mississippi to draw upon the TANF contingency fund. 100% federal funding (no state match required) up to a maximum 70% of the TANF block grant in a year for the 14 months August 2005-September 2006. Also allows these states to draw upon the loan fund, with the maximum loan of 40% of the TANF block grant with the loan and interest on the loan forgiven.
Funding to a state hosting evacuees from directly impacted states	Permits states to draw from the existing TANF contingency fund to pay benefits for evacuees from directly impacted states. Families cannot already be receiving benefits from their home state. 100% federal funding (no match required) for the cost of these benefits up to a maximum 20% of the TANF block grant in the year.	Permits states to draw from the existing TANF contingency fund to pay benefits for evacuees from directly impacted states. 100% federal funding (no match requirement) for the cost of these benefits up to a maximum 70% of the TANF block grant for the 14 months August 2005-September 2005.
Application of TANF requirements to families affected by Hurricane Katrina	Time limits and work requirements do not apply to such families if the benefits are paid as non-recurrent, short-term benefits to meet a subsistence need.	Time limits, work requirements, and certain child support requirements do not apply to evacuated families receiving "Hurricane Katrina Emergency TANF Benefits" provided in other states. "Hurricane Katrina Emergency Benefits" are benefits and services normally provided by TANF that are designated as emergency benefits for evacuated families or families in Alabama, Louisiana, or Mississippi.

Table 2. Continued

Provision	H.R. 3672 (as passed both the House and Senate)	TANF Provisions of S. 1716
TANF Penalties	Waives TANF penalties for Alabama, Louisiana, and Mississippi for failure to comply with TANF requirements. Does not waive the penalty for failure to meet state fiscal effort.	Similar provision.
TANF Funding	Allows states to draw their first quarter FY06 grant (normally payable on October 1, 2005) in Sept. 2005. Extends TANF funding through the end of Dec. 2005.	No change from H.R. 3672.
Use of Unspent TANF Funds	Allows states to use unspent funds for any TANF benefit or service for a family affected by Hurricane Katrina.	No change from H.R. 3672.

Source: Congressional Research Service (CRS).

- Allowing families in the three states directly impacted by Hurricane Katrina and evacuees from those states to receive benefits free of certain TANF requirements, such as the work requirement and time limit.
- Allowing an advance draw down of the first quarter of the FY2006 TANF block grant in September 2005;
- Allowing states to use unspent TANF funds on any benefit and service to aid families affected by the Hurricane; and
- Waiving penalties for failure to comply with most TANF requirements for the states of Alabama, Louisiana, and Mississippi.

Though the Senate passed H.R. 3672 on September 15, 2005 by unanimous consent, that same day Senate Finance Committee Chairman Grassley and Ranking Member Baucus introduced S. 1716, which would amend provisions of H.R. 3672 by increasing the limits and availability of the contingency fund and allowing a waiver of TANF requirements for a broader set of benefits and services. Table 2 compares provisions of H.R. 3672 with those of S. 1716.

REFERENCES

[1] For details on TANF grants and financing, as well as requirements the block grant places on states, see: CRS Report RL32748, *The Temporary Assistance for Needy Families (TANF) Block Grant: A Primer on Financing and Requirements for State Programs.*

[2] The rules for emergency assistance are not in TANF statute, but are in regulations promulgated by the Department of Health and Human Services (HHS) at 45 CFR 260.31.

In: Family Structure and Support Issues   ISBN: 1-60021-340-5
Editor: A. E. Bennett, pp. 27-64   © 2007 Nova Science Publishers, Inc.

Chapter 3

A REVIEW OF MEDICAL CHILD SUPPORT: BACKGROUND, POLICY, AND ISSUES*

Carmen Solomon-Fears

ABSTRACT

Medical child support is the legal provision of payment of medical, dental, prescription, and other health care expenses of dependent children. It can include provisions to cover health insurance costs as well as cash payments for unreimbursed medical expenses. According to 2001 Child Support Enforcement (CSE) data, 93% of medical child support is provided in the form of health insurance coverage. The requirement for medical child support is apart of all child support orders (administered by CSE agencies), and it only pertains to the parent's dependent children. Activities undertaken by CSE agencies to establish and enforce medical child support are eligible for federal reimbursement at the CSE matching rate of 66%.

The medical child support process requires that a state CSE agency *notify* the employer of a noncustodial parent who owes child support, that the parent is obligated to provide health care coverage for his or her dependent children. CSE agencies notify employers of a medical child support order via a standardized federal form called the National Medical Support Notice. The plan administrator must then determine whether family health care coverage is available for which the dependent children may be eligible. If eligible, the plan administrator is required to enroll the dependent child in an appropriate

---

* Excerpted from CRS Report RL32135, dated November 3, 2003.

plan, and notify the noncustodial parent's employer of the premium amount to be withheld from the employee's paycheck.

Although establishment of a medical support order is a prerequisite to enforcing the order, inclusion of a health insurance order does not necessarily mean that health insurance coverage is actually provided. According to CSE program data, in 2001, only 49% of child support orders included health insurance coverage, and the health insurance order was complied with in only 18% of the cases. Most policymakers agree that health care coverage for dependent children must be available, accessible, affordable, and stable. Since 1977 and sporadically through 1998, Congress has passed legislation to help states effectively establish and enforce medical child support. The National Medical Support Notice, mandated by 1998 law and promulgated in March 2001, was viewed as a means to significantly improve enforcement of medical child support — to date only about half the states are using the Notice. The 1998 law also called for an advisory body to design a medical child support incentive which would become part of the CSE performance-based incentive payment system — a recommendation was made to Congress in 2001 to indefinitely delay development of a medical child support incentive mainly because it was argued that the appropriate data was not yet available upon which to base such an incentive.

Improving the establishment and enforcement of medical child support has been hampered to some extent by factors such as high health care costs, a decline in employer-provided health insurance coverage, an increase in the share of health insurance costs borne by employees, and the large number of uninsured children. This chapter provides a legislative history of medical support provisions in the CSE program, describes current policy with respect to medical child support, examines available data, and discusses some of the issues related to medical child support.

BACKGROUND

Most Americans view health care for their children and for themselves as one of their top concerns. The adverse consequences of going without health insurance may include unmet health and dental needs, lower receipt of preventive services, avoidable hospitalizations, increased likelihood of receiving expensive emergency room care, and reduced likelihood that the doctor is familiar with the patient's medical history. From a public health perspective, early and frequent monitoring of children's health is a key component to ensuring the appropriate growth and healthy development of children. From a family perspective, health insurance coverage greatly reduces parental financial and emotional stress. Medical child support benefits families by increasing the incidence of noncustodial parents who obtain private health insurance coverage for their dependent children. With medical child support, Congress found a way to make noncustodial parents responsible for their children and lessen taxpayer burden by shifting costs from the taxpayers back to the noncustodial parents.

Since 1977, Congress has tried to offset some of the costs associated with the Medicaid program by allowing states to require Medicaid recipients to assign their child support rights to the state and allowing the state to pursue reimbursement of the cost of Medicaid benefits provided to the child from the child's noncustodial parent (in 1984 mandatory assignment became law). Since 1984, Congress has tried to increase provision of private health care coverage for children whose noncustodial parent has access to employer-related or group health insurance that is provided at a reasonable cost. This is seen as a way to make noncustodial parents responsible for their children and lessen taxpayer burden by shifting costs from the taxpayers back to the noncustodial parents. For a detailed legislative history, see Appendix A.

In 1984, federal law required that state Child Support Enforcement (CSE) agencies petition for the inclusion of medical support as part of any child support order whenever health care coverage is available to the noncustodial parent at reasonable cost. A 1993 amendment to the Employee Retirement Income Security Act (ERISA) required employer-sponsored group health plans to extend health care coverage to the children of a parent/employee who is divorced, separated, or never married when ordered to do so by the state CSE agency via a Qualified Medical Child Support Order (QMCSO). The 1996 welfare reform law further strengthened medical support by stipulating that all orders enforced by the state CSE agency must include a provision for health care coverage.[1] The 1996 law also directed the CSE agency to notify the noncustodial parent's employer of the employee's medical child support obligation. To help obtain health care coverage for children, a 1998 law authorized the creation of the National Medical Support Notice (NMSN), a standardized form, that is the exclusive document which must be used by all state CSE agencies. An appropriately completed NMSN is considered to be a "Qualified Medical Child Support Order," and as such must be honored by the noncustodial parent's employer's group health plan.

The reader should recognize that efforts to improve the establishment and enforcement of medical child support need to be viewed in the current context of high health care costs, a decline in employer-provided health insurance coverage (which is the foundation of the current medical child support system), an increase in the share of health insurance costs borne by employees, and a large number of children who are uninsured. Moreover, cash support and medical support are not always compatible. For example, if premiums, co-payments, and deductibles of noncustodial parents rise, fairness might suggest that the cash child support payment of noncustodial parents be reduced to reflect payment of additional medical costs. The result, however, would be that custodial parents would have less income to provide for the basic food, clothing, and shelter needs of their dependent children; conversely, if medical support is not available, the family will undoubtedly face dire economic circumstances if a child becomes seriously ill.

The public and policymakers generally agree that establishment and enforcement of medical support, where it is available on reasonable terms, promotes family responsibility, improves children's access to health care, and usually saves federal and state dollars. This chapter provides a legislative history of medical support provisions in the CSE program, describes current policy with respect to medical child support, examines data on medical child support, and discusses some of the issues related to medical child support.

CURRENT POLICY

Federal law mandates that states have procedures under which all child support orders are required to include a provision for the health care coverage of the child (section 466(a)(19) of the Social Security Act). Medical support is the legal provision of payment of medical, dental, prescription, and other health care expenses for dependent children by the noncustodial parent. It can include provisions to cover health insurance costs as well as cash payments for unreimbursed medical expenses. The requirement for medical child support is a part of the child support order, and it only pertains to the parent's dependent children. The reader should note that states can establish child support orders (and thereby medical child support orders) either by a judicial or administrative process (i.e., through the state courts or through the state CSE agencies). Activities undertaken by the state CSE agencies to establish and enforce medical support are eligible for federal reimbursement at the general CSE matching rate of 66%.[2]

Medical support can take several forms. The noncustodial parent may be ordered to: (1) provide health insurance if available through his or her employer, (2) pay for private health insurance (health care coverage) premiums or reimburse the custodial parent for all or a portion of the costs of health insurance obtained by the custodial parent for the child, or (3) pay additional amounts to cover some or all of ongoing medical bills as reimbursement for uninsured medical costs.[3]

National Census Data
1999 — 56% of child support orders included health insurance coverage; parents complied with 49% of these health insurance orders
CSE Program Data
2001 — 49% of child support orders included health insurance coverage; parents complied with 49% of these health insurance orders

Congress has realized for many years that medical support enforcement activities need to be strengthened. Congress recognized early in the implementation of the CSE program that many noncustodial parents had private health insurance coverage available through employers, unions or other groups and that such coverage could be extended when available at reasonable cost to provide for dependents' medical expenses. The medical child support provisions benefit families by increasing the incidence of noncustodial parents who obtain health insurance coverage for their dependent children. Moreover, the medical child support provisions result in cost savings to states and the federal governments by reducing Medicaid expenditures when such health care insurance is available to families who are eligible for Medicaid services.[4]

According to federal regulations (45 CFR 303.31), for both families who have assigned their medical support rights to the state and families who have applied for CSE services, the CSE agency must:

1. Petition the court or administrative authority to include in the child support order health insurance that is available to the noncustodial parent at reasonable cost in new or modified child support orders, unless the child has satisfactory health insurance other than Medicaid;
2. Petition the court or administrative authority to include medical support whether or not — (a) health insurance at reasonable cost is actually available to the noncustodial parent at the time the order is entered; or (b) modification of current coverage to include the child(ren) in question is immediately possible;
3. Establish written criteria to identify cases not included under the previous two provisions where there is a high potential for obtaining medical support based on — (a) evidence that health insurance may be available to the noncustodial parent at a reasonable cost, and (b) facts, as defined by state law, regulation, procedure, or other directive, which are

sufficient to warrant modification of the existing support order to include health insurance coverage for a dependent child(ren);

4. Petition the court or administrative authority to modify child support orders for cases that are likely to have access to health insurance to include medical support in the form of health insurance coverage;

5. Provide the custodial parent with information pertaining to the health insurance policy which has been secured for the dependent child(ren);

6. Inform the Medicaid agency when a new or modified court or administrative order for child support includes medical support and provide specific information to the Medicaid agency when the information is available;

7. If health insurance is available to the noncustodial parent at reasonable cost and has not been obtained at the time the order is entered, take steps to enforce the health insurance coverage required by the support order and provide the Medicaid agency with the necessary information;

8. Periodically communicate with the Medicaid agency to determine if there have been lapses in health insurance coverage for Medicaid applicants and recipients; and

9. Request employers and other groups offering health insurance coverage that is being enforced by the CSE agency to notify the CSE agency of lapses in coverage.

In addition, a medical child support order must contain the following information in order to be *"qualified"*: (1) the name and last known mailing address of the participant and each child covered by the order, except that the order may substitute the name and mailing address of a state or local official for the mailing address of any child covered by the order; (2) a reasonable description of the type of health coverage to be provided (or the manner in which such coverage is to be determined); and (3) the period to which the order applies.

To help obtain health care coverage for children, a 1998 law authorized the creation of the NMSN. The NMSN is a standardized federal form that all state CSE agencies are supposed to use when issuing a medical support order to employers. An appropriately completed NMSN is considered to be a "Qualified Medical Child Support Order," and as such must be honored by the noncustodial parent's employer's group health plan.[5]

Cash child support collections by CSE agencies are distributed in several ways, including in the form of medical support. They may be sent to the family, divided between the state and federal governments, used as incentive payments to states, or used for medical support (and sent to the Medicaid agency or the family). For FY2001, total child support collections were distributed as follows: 87.7% went to families; 5.3% went to the states; 4.7% went to the federal government; 1.8% were paid out as incentive payments to states; and 0.5% was paid as medical support. To the extent that medical support has been assigned to the state, medical support collections are forwarded to the Medicaid agency for distribution. Otherwise, the amount collected as medical support is forwarded to the family.[6] (It should be noted that the provision of medical support in the form of health insurance coverage is not quantified in the above data.)

In general, health insurance is preferred over other types of medical support because it usuallyis relativelyinexpensive for the employee/noncustodial parent (due to the employer contribution), it is easier for the CSE agency to monitor, and it can cover children who otherwise would be dependent on Medicaid benefits (at taxpayer expense).[7] In FY2001, medical support orders were issued in the form of health insurance in 93% of the cases that included a medical support order (see Table 2). The conference report on the Child Support Enforcement Amendments of 1984 (which became P.L. 98-378) stated:

"... the conferees believe that the best long run solution to achieving medical insurance coverage for all families is the use of private medical insurance which is or can be made available through a parent's employer."[8]

The medical child support process requires that a state CSE agency issue a notice to the employer of a noncustodial parent, who is subject to a child support order issued by a court or administrative agency, informing the employer of the parent's obligation to provide health care coverage for the child(ren). The employer must then determine whether family health care coverage is available for which the dependent child(ren) may be eligible, and if so, the employer must notify the plan administrator of each plan covered by the National Medical Support Notice. If the dependent child(ren) is eligible for coverage under a plan, the plan administrator is required to enroll the dependent child(ren) in an appropriate plan. The plan administrator also must notify the noncustodial parent's employer of the premium amount to be withheld from the employee's paycheck.[9]

MEDICAL CHILD SUPPORT DATA

This section examines data from three different sources: national data from the U.S. Census Bureau, state CSE program data from the federal Office of Child

Support Enforcement (OCSE), and longitudinal data from the Survey of Income and Program Participation. All of the data indicate that much more needs to be done to improve the establishment and enforcement of medical support, in accordance with current law. In reviewing the data, it is important to note that (1) in some cases children did not receive a child support award of any kind, cash or medical care; (2) even if there was a cash award, in many cases, health insurance coverage was not included in the award; and (3) even when health insurance coverage was included, in many cases, it was not actually provided by the noncustodial parent.

Census Data

The U.S. Census Bureau periodically collects national survey information on child support. The Census Bureau interviews a random sample of single-parent families to gather data that can be used to assess the performance of noncustodial parents in paying child support and providing health insurance coverage. The Census data are based on all single-parent families in the United States with children under age 21 who are living apart from their other parent. The Census data are more comprehensive than CSE program data but do not disaggregate the data on a state-by-state basis.

Figure 1 displays data obtained from April supplements to the Census Bureau's Current Population Survey. These supplements provide information on the receipt of child support payments by parents living with their own children whose other parent is not living with the family. Figure 1 only displays information from cases in which the mother is the custodial parent.[10] Figure 1 indicates that during the period from 1989-1999, the percentage of child support awards that included health insurance increased from 40.1% to 55.6%. Thus, in 1999 about 56% of mothers awarded child support payments had health insurance included in their award. This coincides with congressional efforts to make health care coverage part of the child support obligation. However, the examination of enforcement, i.e., whether health insurance was actually provided, shows a different picture. During the 1989-1999 period, the percentage of child support awards that included health insurance in which health insurance coverage was actually provided by the father dropped almost 28%, from 67.6% in 1989 to 48.9% in 1999. Thus, in 1999, only 49% of custodial mothers expecting to receive health benefits for their children actually did so.

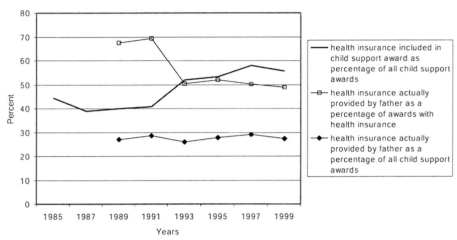

Source: Prepared by the Congressional Research Service based on data from Census Bureau reports.

Figure 1. Health Insurance and Child Support Awards.

The third trend line in Figure 1 looks at cases in which health insurance was actually provided by the father as a percentage of all cases in which child support was awarded (as opposed to just those that included health insurance). It shows a relatively flat line. In other words, during the period 1989-1999, the percentage of cases in which health insurance was required to be provided by the father relative to all cases in which child support was awarded remained relatively unchanged. The percentage was 27.1% in 1989, it jumped to 28.5% in 1991, dropped back to 26.1% in 1993, rose to 27.7% in 1995 and to 29.1% in 1997, and dropped back to 27.2% in 1999. Thus, even though there were some gains in the requirement for provision of health insurance, the actual provision of health insurance to children living with their custodial mothers did not improve much over the 1989-1999 period.

Table 1 provides detailed information for 1999, the most recent year for which national data are available, on the inclusion of the father's health insurance in orders received by families headed by mothers. Although the 1999 survey, like the 1997, 1995, 1993, and 1991 surveys, included custodial fathers, the table and following discussion are focused solely on custodial mothers. While indicating that about 56% of all mothers have health insurance included in their child support award, the table also shows that the probability of health insurance coverage is greatly reduced for never-married women (39%), black (42%) and Hispanic women (42%), and women with less schooling (i.e., high school dropouts, 36%).

**Table 1. Child Support Award Status and Inclusion of Health Insurance
in Child Support Award, by Selected Characteristics
of Custodial Mothers, 1999**

Characteristic of custodial mothers	Total (thousands)	Supposed to receive child support payments in 1999		
		Total (thousands)	Health insurance included in child support award	
			Number (thousands)	Percent of total awarded
Current marital status:ᵃ				
Married	2,588	1,568	1,129	62.8%
Divorced	3,760	2,448	1,753	63.2
Separated	1,329	602	361	49.4
Never married	3,698	1,464	692	38.7
Race/Hispanic origin:ᵇ				
White	7,858	4,621	3,189	59.9
Black	3,225	1,289	663	42.4
Hispanic	1,728	717	360	42.2
Age:				
15-17 years	83	7	6	21.4
18-29 years	3,344	1,499	822	46.3
30-39 years	4,433	2,554	1,604	55.3
40 years or older	3,368	2,073	1,547	63.2
Years of school completed:				
Less than high school graduate	2,239	888	406	35.8
High school graduate or GED	4,344	2,229	1,463	55.4
Some college, no degree	2,536	1,524	1,051	61.6
Associate degree	1,013	616	411	58.8
Bachelors degree or more	1,367	877	648	66.7
Number of own children present from an absent father:				
One child	6,527	3,065	1,978	53.7
Two children	3,367	2,118	1,425	60.7
Three children	1,099	667	425	54.7
Four children or more	507	282	150	44.0
Total	11,499	6,133	3,978	55.6

Source: U.S. Census Bureau. 2002.

Note: Custodial mothers are defined as women 15 years and older with children under
  21 years of age present from absent fathers as of Spring 2000.

ᵃ Excludes a small number of currently widowed women whose previous marriage
  ended in divorce.

ᵇ. Persons of Hispanic origin may be of any race.

CSE Program Data

The medical support provisions appear to be having an impact on the number of children in single-parent families with medical coverage in their child support orders. According to CSE program data, which reflect welfare families who are automatically eligible for CSE services and nonwelfare families who have applied for CSE services, 49% of child support orders in FY2001 included health insurance coverage, up from 35% in FY1991. Although the CSE system has been making progress in including health insurance coverage in child support orders, these figures indicate that many children still lack health insurance coverage.

Percentage of Child Support Awards Enforced or Modified that Include a Health Insurance Order			
FY1991	35.3%	FY1997	38.9%
FY1992	30.0%	FY1998	34.8%
FY1993	29.7%	FY1999	42.7%
FY1994	32.3%	FY2000	47.0%
FY1995	32.7%	FY2001	49.3%
FY1996	34.2%		

P.L. 105-200 required the Secretary of the Department of Health and Human Services (HHS) to submit a report to Congress containing recommendations on a medical support indicator and its integration with the new performance-based incentive funding system established for the federal Child Support Enforcement program. The Medical Support Incentive Work Group (MSIWG), which was formed pursuant to this mandate, recommended in 2000 that a medical support performance measure be delayed because of the lack of reliable historical information on medical support. Three of the data elements suggested by the group are now part of the data-reporting form OCSE-157 that states are required to complete. The three elements are: (1) cases where medical support is ordered (includes cash medical support and/or health insurance coverage); (2) cases where health insurance specifically is ordered; and (3) cases where health insurance is provided as ordered. These data elements appear in Table 2.

Table 2 shows that in FY2001, only 5.452 million (49%) of the 11.050 million families with child support orders had an order that included health insurance. The inclusion of health insurance in child support orders varied considerably from state to state, from a high of 100% in South Carolina and 83% in Idaho to a low of 2.1% in the District of Columbia and 10% in Kansas.

Table 2. Medical Child Support, FY2001

States	CSE cases with child support orders	CSE cases with medical support order	Health insurance included	Health insurance provided	Health insurance included as % of CSE orders	Health insurance provided as % of health insurance orders
Alabama	172,951	87,714	86,675	599	50.1%	0.7%
Alaska	36,532	29,623	29,591	9,378	81.0	31.7
Arizona	140,993	51,284	50,974	808	36.2	1.6
Arkansas	103,633	70,447	56,424	9,558	54.4	16.9
California	1,409,690	1,019,147	964,951	218,067	68.5	22.6
Colorado	112,463	71,958	71,951	5,960	64.0	8.3
Connecticut	125,622	74,928	74,884	12,508	59.6	16.7
Dist. of Columbia	31,795	22,637	660	-	2.1	0.0
Florida	391,027	94,854	78,550	2,813	20.1	3.6
Georgia	313,807	1,710	107,208	20,043	34.2	18.7
Guam	5,909	3,928	3,910	438	66.2	11.2
Hawaii	55,424	17,853	17,801	2,385	32.1	13.4
Idaho	57,991	48,215	48,158	5,274	83.0	11.0
Illinois	36,386	96,577	95,752	25,927	28.5	27.1
Indiana	244,552	217	57,669	644	23.6	1.1
Iowa	145,054	92,601	91,964	21,098	63.4	22.9
Kansas	85,602	9,568	8,629	791	10.1	9.2
Kentucky	204,658	74,662	68,710	3,430	33.6	5.0
Louisiana	166,596	126,718	126,685	702	76.0	0.6
Maine	55,868	36,359	23,143	1,034	41.4	4.5
Maryland	211,504	96,604	96,029	37,653	45.4	39.2
Massachusetts	166,329	40,572	40,568	917	24.4	2.3
Michigan	762,254	424,451	380,402	60,352	49.9	15.9
Minnesota	180,678	131,199	101,441	36,277	56.1	35.8
Mississippi	139,287	62,077	37,404	6,794	26.9	18.2
Missouri	294,127	207,674	204,314	24,619	69.5	12.0
Montana	30,217	24,184	24,001	6,489	79.4	27.0
Nebraska	72,875	22,180	22,132	-	30.4	0.0
Nevada	56,635	41,117	40,284	2,142	71.1	5.3
New Hampshire	30,497	21,065	18,209	1,698	59.7	9.3
New Jersey	267,107	147,156	147,036	41,203	55.0	28.0
New Mexico	29,837	17,255	17,226	-	57.7	0.0
New York	661,395	280,175	267,221	-	40.4	0.0

Table 2. Continued

States	CSE cases with child support orders	CSE cases with medical support order	Health insurance included	Health insurance provided	Health insurance included as % of CSE orders	Health insurance provided as % of health insurance orders
North Carolina	303,751	183,036	179,548	56,508	59.1	31.5
North Dakota	24,140	22,802	19,025	7,759	78.8	40.8
Ohio	625,300	279,339	103,454	88,535	16.5	85.6
Oklahoma	94,469	75,426	72,613	-	76.9	0.0
Oregon	161,157	118,119	118,119	26,245	73.3	22.2
Pennsylvania	489,726	171,116	122,438	37,858	25.0	30.9
Puerto Rico	146,368	51	43	16	0.0	37.2
Rhode Island	32,829	20,082	20,081	3,918	61.2	19.5
South Carolina	149,464	150,088	150,081	12,531	100.4	8.3
South Dakota	25,888	19,042	19,042	4,123	73.6	21.7
Tennessee	195,714	105,104	88,455	12,457	45.2	14.1
Texas	633,327	483,489	468,772	31,752	74.0	6.8
Utah	63,862	57,437	4,909	21,559	70.3	48.0
Vermont	21,557	9,225	9,218	7,011	42.8	76.1
Virgin Islands	-	-	-	-	-	-
Virginia	283,587	150,318	150,218	13,100	53.0	8.7
Washington	278,674	18,355	217,606	56,012	78.1	25.7
West Virginia	85,450	44,517	29,314	2,106	34.3	7.2
Wisconsin	266,665	146,967	145,127	31,104	54.4	21.4
Wyoming	31,246	16,706	10,349	1,427	33.1	13.8
Total	11,049,610	5,840,197	5,452,220	976,387	49.3%	17.9%

Source: Table prepared by the Congressional Research Service based on data from the Office of Child Support Enforcement.

Moreover, only 18% of health insurance orders actually resulted in health benefits. In other words, in 2001, only 18% of custodial families expecting to receive health benefits for their children actually did so. Again, there was wide variation by state; in Ohio health insurance was provided as ordered in 86% of the cases that included a health insurance order; the comparable figure in Vermont was 76%. At the other end of the spectrum, nine states reported that less than 2% of the cases that included a health insurance order actually provided health insurance coverage.

SIPP Data

A report prepared in 2000 by the Urban Institute provides longitudinal data on the health care coverage of children living with their mothers (and apart from their fathers). The report is based on analysis of the 1993 Survey of Income and Program Participation (SIPP), a longitudinal survey containing detailed income and demographic information on a nationally representative sample of approximately 20,000 households. Two tables from the report are presented in Appendix B.

Table B.1 shows that 37% of the child support awards ordered in 1993 included an award of health insurance coverage by the noncustodial father, 16% required the custodial parent to provide coverage, 9% made some other provision for medical costs such as requiring the noncustodial parent to pay medical costs directly or including cash medical support in the child support award. Thirty-eight percent (38%) of child support awards ordered in 1993 included no provision for health care coverage of any kind.

Table B.2 examines the health care coverage of custodial children based on whether the noncustodial father was required to provide health care coverage for his dependent children. The second panel of Table B.2 provides information on the health care coverage status of custodial families in which the father was ordered to provide health care coverage for his dependent children. It shows that 68% of the custodial families reported receiving health care coverage from the noncustodial father in at least one month of 1993, 17% reported the use of the custodial parent's health insurance to provide health care for the children, 11% relied exclusively on Medicaid or Medicare, and 4% were uninsured. Sixty-five percent of the custodial families reported that the private coverage from the noncustodial father or custodial mother was valid for all 12 months of the year.

The author of the report made the following remarks regarding the current applicability of the 1993 findings.

The results presented in this paper are based on data from 1993, the most recent year for which information on nonresident fathers is readily available. To what extent have changes since 1993 affected nonresident fathers' ability to provide health care coverage? If nonresident fathers have experienced the same health care coverage trends as the overall workforce, then the flattening out of several health care coverage trends since 1993 suggests that the findings are still relevant.[11]

Although SIPP also collected information on health insurance coverage of custodial children in its 2001 topical module questionnaire, those data are not yet available.

Data Summary

The national Census Bureau data, which reflect the universe of custodial families, show that in 1999 about 56% of mothers awarded child support payments had health insurance included in their child support award. It also showed that only 49% (i.e., 49% of the 56%) of custodial mothers expecting to receive health benefits for their children actually did so. In contrast, the CSE program data, which reflect welfare families who are automatically eligible for CSE services and nonwelfare families who have applied for CSE services, show that in FY2001 about 49% of child support awards included a health insurance order. Further, only 18% of health insurance orders were provided as ordered (i.e., only 18% of custodial mothers expecting to receive health benefits for their children actually did so).

The CSE program data show a less effective medical support effort than the national Census Bureau data. This may be because noncustodial parents that are not part of the CSE program have more income and are more able to provide medical support for their children. Even so, as noted earlier, the national data also indicate that much more needs to be accomplished with regard to establishment and enforcement of medical support.

Establishment of Health Insurance Order as Part of Child Support Award/Order

As noted, the CSE program data indicate that in 2001, only 49% of families with child support awards had a health insurance order included as part of their child support award/order. An HHS IG report released in June 2000 found "*child support agencies deficient in pursuing health insurance availability...*" The report noted that CSE staff indicated that while they do try to obtain employment and health insurance information pertaining to noncustodial parents, they believe their primary efforts should be spent in obtaining cash child support payments.[12] Some observers contend that medical support provisions should be expanded to require both noncustodial and custodial parents to disclose information about actual and potential private health care coverage to help CSE agencies better and/or more quickly determine whether private health insurance coverage is available to the dependent children. Also, during the last several years there has been a decline in the number of employers that provides health insurance for their employees (which is the foundation of the current medical child support system), and among employers who do provide health insurance, the share of health insurance costs borne by employees has increased.

Enforcement of Health Insurance Order

Of perhaps more significance is the fact that only 18% of CSE families with a health insurance order included in their child support award actually received the health care coverage mandated by the order (2001 data). Clearly, enforcement of the health insurance order can only come after the health insurance order has been established. However, higher enforcement levels are not necessarily correlated to higher levels of establishment of health insurance coverage.

Some reasons for the low compliance with health insurance orders may be that the health care coverage is not (1) affordable — health care costs have risen dramatically over the last decade and those costs have in many instances been passed on to the beneficiary, so that noncustodial parents who can no longer meet the premium fees, co-payments, deductibles, and other costs associated with the coverage and may let the coverage lapse or terminate the coverage altogether; (2) accessible — the rise in the use of Health Maintenance Organizations to deliver health insurance coverage has led to many cases in which the dependent child is not in the HMO service area and therefore not eligible for coverage; (3) stability — not all workers are full-time, year-round employees, thus in the cases of temporary or seasonal workers, any access they had to health care coverage would generally end when their employment ended.

ISSUES

To improve establishment and enforcement of medical child support, there are a range of health coverage options. Generally speaking for the last several years the focus has been on obtaining private health care coverage exclusively from noncustodial parents. The extent to which custodial parents work and have access to employer-sponsored health insurance has increased significantly during the last 20 years. Similarly, Medicaid coverage based on child poverty has also increased. Today, in many cases health care coverage is more accessible if it is based on the custodial parent's coverage.[13] Moreover, over the last several years health care costs have dramatically increased, and it can no longer be assumed that all employer-sponsored health insurance is affordable. Requiring and enforcing expensive health care insurance may negatively affect the custodial parent and child as well as the noncustodial parent. Most policymakers agree that health care coverage must be available, accessible, affordable, and stable. Observers state that if the goal is to reduce the number of uninsured children with child support orders, in some cases, the only way to obtain this result will be to rely on publicly-funded health care.

As indicated by the data discussed earlier, federal law has not been fully effective in addressing medical child support. However, two provisions of federal law have yet to be fully implemented. P.L. 105-200 stipulated that a medical child support incentive payment system be developed — that has not yet happened. Further, although the National Medical Support Notice was promulgated December 27, 2000 and became effective on March 27, 2001, as discussed below, only half of the states are using it.

The discussion below provides context and background to some of the issues that are preventing states from effectively establishing and enforcing medical child support.

Slow Progress in Establishing and Enforcing Medical Support

As mentioned elsewhere in this chapter, the 1984 law (P.L. 98-378) basically requires CSE agencies to secure medical support information, and to secure and enforce medical support obligations whenever health care coverage is available to the noncustodial parent at a reasonable cost. Recognizing that states were making slow progress in establishing and enforcing medical support, Congress in the 1993 amendments (P.L. 103-66) sought to remove some of the barriers to effective medical support enforcement. The 1993 law prohibited discriminatory health care coverage practices, created "qualified medical child support orders" to obtain coverage from group health plans that were covered by the Employee Retirement Income Security Act (ERISA), and allowed employers to deduct the costs of health insurance premiums from the employee/obligor's paycheck. Even with the enactment of the 1996 welfare reform law (P.L. 104-193), which required inclusion of health care coverage in all child support orders established or enforced by CSE agencies, it is generally agreed that the establishment and enforcement of medical support has remained inadequate.

A 1998 law (P.L. 105-200) required the development and use of a "National Medical Support Notice" and also established a Medical Child Support Working Group charged with making recommendations to overcome the barriers to effective enforcement of medical support.[14] The Working Group submitted a report to the Secretaries of the Departments of Health and Human Services (HHS) and Labor in June 2000 containing 76 recommendations related to medical child support. These recommendations have not been considered by Congress.

Although some critics claim that much more needs to be accomplished with regard to the provision of medical support for children receiving CSE services, some analysts contend that the federal government has made tremendous strides. They note the following accomplishments. The federal government has moved from recoupment of Medicaid costs to pursuit of private medical support. The federal government has moved from simply petitioning for medical support to requiring that medical support be included in all CSE orders. The federal government has moved from simply establishing medical support to requiring a uniform national medical support notice that must be honored by employer group health plans. They conclude that the 19-year period from 1984-2003 encompasses much progress in both establishing medical support orders and in enforcing those orders.

Some proponents advocate the collection of medical support through income withholding. They assert that child support and medical support should be fully integrated and enforced primarily through income withholding. They point out that income withholding as a percentage of all child support collections went from about 50% right before automatic income withholding was mandated in 1994 to 65% of collections in FY2002. They contend that just as income withholding has been so successful for cash child support, so too could medical support benefit from the mandatory use of income withholding.[15] Others warn that income withholding is too intrusive and does not account for changing financial circumstances. They also contend that the combination of both child support and medical support may exceed the limits imposed by the Consumer Credit Protection Act.[16]

Examining the Health Care Coverage of Both Parents

According to federal regulations [45 CFR 303.31(b)(1)], if the custodial parent is already providing satisfactory private health care coverage for herself and the children, state CSE agencies are not required to petition the court or administrative agency to include private health insurance coverage that is available to the noncustodial parent at reasonable cost in new or modified child support orders. This means that if the custodial parent is bearing the full cost of premiums, co-payments and deductibles — without assistance from the noncustodial parent — the CSE agency will take no action. In such cases, cash child support may be used to pay health care costs. In some cases, a child may have private health care coverage but live in poor housing or lack adequate food or clothing.[17] Some observers argue that health insurance should be an adjunct to, not a substitute for, the noncustodial parent's obligation to provide financial support for his or her child; they note that when insurance costs are subtracted from the noncustodial parent's financial obligation, the custodial parent has less resources to spend in the best interest of the child.[18] Others argue that when medical child support is not provided, the custodial parents may not be able to oversee the medical health of their children.

According to the Medical Child Support Working Group, it often is assumed that only the noncustodial parent has access to private health insurance. It cites a number of statistics that affirms this is a fallacy. It recommends that a new paradigm should be adopted in which coverage available to both parents is examined in determining the medical support obligation. Under this paradigm, if only the custodial parent has coverage, that coverage should be ordered and the noncustodial parent should contribute toward the cost of such coverage. When both parents are potentially able to provide coverage, the coverage available through the custodial parent (with a contribution toward the cost by the noncustodial parent) should normally be preferred because it — (1) most likely is accessible to the child, (2) involves less difficultyin claims processing for the custodial parent, the provider, and the insurer, and (3) minimizes the enforcement difficulties of the CSE agency or private attorney responsible for the case.[19]

Some analysts caution that this policy may cause conflict if the state has to enforce a medical support order against the custodial parent, especially if the custodial parent contends that the reason the medical obligation was unmet was because the noncustodial parent failed to make his or her contribution. Such conflict may occur because there is much confusion over whom the CSE attorney represents. Most custodial parents believe that the CSE agency represents them when in fact the CSE agency represents the state.

Accessibility of Health Care Coverage

In general, private health care coverage that is available to the *custodial* parent usually is accessible to the child even if the plan coverage has a limited service area, as is the case with many Health Maintenance Organizations (HMOs). However, this may *not* be the case when it is the *noncustodial* parent whose health insurance coverage is being used, particularly if that coverage is provided through an HMO.[20] Thus, for children living far from their noncustodial parent, managed care reduces the attractiveness of coverage under the noncustodial parent's plan relative to other options for health care coverage. For example, HMO coverage in California may be useless to a child living in Massachusetts. Likewise, coverage available in upstate New York may be too far away to be useful to a child living in New York City. According to one report, since managed care is now the norm and only 40% of noncustodial fathers live in the same city or county as their children, this can be a serious problem.[21]

Under the Medical Child Support Working Group's paradigm, when private health care coverage is available to a child, the CSE agency should consider the accessibility of covered services before it decides to pursue the coverage. According to the Working Group, children should not be enrolled in any plan whose services/providers are not accessible to them, unless the plan can provide financial reimbursement for services rendered by alternate providers.[22]

The Working Group recommended that federal regulations be developed to define "accessible" coverage and that it be made clear that coverage that is not accessible should not be ordered. The Working Group reported the following with regard to a definition of "accessible":

> Coverage is accessible if the covered children can obtain services from a plan provider with reasonable effort by the custodial parent. When the only health care option available to the noncustodial parent is a plan that limits service coverage to providers within a defined geographic area, the decision maker should determine whether the child lives within the plan's service area. If the child does not live within the plan's service area, the decision maker should determine whether the plan has a reciprocal agreement that permits the child to receive coverage at no greater cost than if the child resided in the plan's service area. The decision maker should also determine if primary care is available within the lesser of 30 minutes or 30 miles of the child's residence. If primary care is not available within these constraints, the coverage should be deemed inaccessible.[23]

In addition, the Medical Child Support Working Group cautioned that to be deemed accessible, the health care coverage also should be stable. The Working Group maintained that the decision maker should base accessibilitypartlyon whether it can reasonably be expected that the health care coverage will remain effective for at least one year, based on the employment history of the parent who is to provide the coverage. In other words, it is the Working Group's opinion that it might not always be feasible to pursue health insurance coverage in the case of parents who are seasonal workers. Some observers contend that if noncustodial parents cannot provide continuous health care coverage for their dependent children, it may be in the best interest of the child to receive private health care coverage from the custodial parent or coverage from Medicaid or the State Children's Health Insurance Program (SCHIP) Under SCHIP, which was established in 1997, low-income children may be better off without any coverage from the noncustodial parent, if that parent is unable to provide continuous coverage because some states do not grant SCHIP eligibility until children have been uninsured for a waiting period of three or more months.[24]

Incentives for Seeking Medical Support

As noted earlier, the federal government provides 66% of the funding for most CSE program activities, including those related to medical support. In order to receive any federal funding, states and/or local governments must provide 34% of the funds needed to operate their CSE programs. In the past, when Congress wanted to encourage activity in an area it considered vital to the effectiveness of the CSE program, it offered federal financial participation (FFP) at a higher than normal level. For example, Congress provided enhanced FFP to encourage paternityestablishment and automation in the CSE program.[25]

The Medical Child Support Working Group contends that Congress should provide enhanced FFP at a 90% rate for medical child support activities to encourage states to more aggressively pursue medical support enforcement. The Working Group's recommendation limits the 90% matching requirement for medical support to 5 years.

P.L. 105-200 (enacted in 1998) also required the HHS Secretary, in consultation with state CSE directors and representatives of children potentially eligible for medical support, to develop a new medical support incentive measure based on the state's effectiveness in establishing and enforcing medical child support obligations. The medical support incentive was to be part of the new revenue-neutral performance-based child support incentive system, established for the overall program in 1998. The 1998 law required that a report on this new incentive measure be submitted to Congress not later than October 1, 1999. According to the House report on the legislation:

> Several witnesses who appeared before the Committee recommended that we consider including medical child support as a performance measure. After discussion, the Committee decided not to include this measure because of the lack of information about the reliability of state data on medical support as well as lack of historical information about state performance on the measure that could be used to estimate payments. However, because medical support is of central importance to a good child support system, the Committee

decided to ask the Secretary to study the feasibility of using medical support as a performance measure and to report her findings to Congress.[26]

Pursuant to this mandate, the HHS Secretary formed the Medical Support Incentive Work Group (MSIWG).[27] The work group met twice over a period of nine months to make recommendations to the Secretary. The work group recommended that the development of the medical support incentive be delayed until 2001 so that it could obtain the necessary data and develop an appropriate measure. This recommendation was included in the Secretary's report to Congress.

A reconstituted MSIWG was later convened and — in September 2001 — recommended that the HHS Secretary not develop a medical support performance measure for incorporation into the existing CSE incentive payment system. Again noting the lack of data, the second MSIWG recommended that a measure be developed, but not for incentive payment purposes. To date, the HHS Secretary has not acted on this report. Hence, a recommendation to Congress has not been made and there remains no incentive payment for medical support activities.

What is Meant by "Reasonable Cost"?

CSE agencies are required to pursue private family health coverage whenever it is available at reasonable cost. Federal regulations state that "health insurance is considered reasonable in cost if it is employment-related or other group health insurance." The definition deeming employment-related coverage or group (e.g., union) health insurance policies to be per se reasonable in cost was first promulgated in 1985. It was justified by a 1983 study by the National Center for Health Services Research, which found that employers paid 72% of the premium cost for low-wage employees. The federal Office of Child Support Enforcement (OCSE) thus concluded that most employment-related or other group health insurance is inexpensive to the employee/noncustodial parent. Rising health care costs have changed the picture. Recent research indicates that the required employee contribution for health care coverage represents a much larger share of familyincome for low-income workers. Some data suggest that on average, employee contributions to family health care coverage premiums are equal to 45% to 52% of the typical cash child support payment.[28]

Although federal regulations (45 CFR section 302.56) require that child support guidelines "provide for the child(ren)'s health care needs, through health insurance coverage or some other means," they do not stipulate how this is to be done. In practice, integrating child support and medical support can be difficult. Most states operate under the position that if the custodial parent provides the health care coverage, the cash support award is suppose to increase, to reflect some contribution from the noncustodial parent toward the cost. If the noncustodial parent provides the coverage, the cash support award is suppose to decrease, to reflect the fact that the noncustodial parent is subsidizing the cost of health care coverage through a separate deduction from wages toward the premium. The results may be problematic in that if the premium associated with the health care coverage is too high, cash support will be substantially reduced, leaving the custodial parent without enough money to take care of the child's food, clothing, and shelter needs. If cash support is not adjusted downward, however, poorer noncustodial parents will pay an unreasonably high portion of their income as support.[29]

Under the Medical Child Support Working Group's paradigm, in deciding whether to pursue private coverage, the cost of coverage should be considered. To the maximum extent possible, public dollars (through, for example, enrollment in Medicaid or the State Children's Health Insurance Program (SCHIP) should be the payment of last resort. Moreover, according to the Working Group, private insurance should not be ordered when its cost significantly lowers the amount of cash child support available to meet the child's basic needs and the child is eligible for some other form of coverage.[30]

According to a Policy Interpretation Questions memorandum,[31] issued by the Office of Child Support Enforcement, concerning "reasonable cost" of medical support, states in which the child support order is established by the courts can enact statutes governing their courts that define "reasonable cost" in a way that the state deems appropriate and still meet federal requirements. For example, under the Texas statute (Section 154.181(e) of the Texas Family Code) "reasonable cost" means the cost of a health insurance premium that does not exceed 10% of the responsible parent's monthly net income.

In contrast, states that set the child support order administratively through their CSE agencies would be subject to federal law and regulations, which stipulate that health insurance is considered reasonable in cost if it is employment-related or other group health insurance.

The Working Group recommended that federal policy be changed to reflect the view that if the cost of providing private health insurance coverage does not exceed 5% of the gross income of the parent who provides coverage, then the cost should be deemed reasonable, regardless of whether the child support order was established by the courts or administratively by the state CSE agency.[32]

Cooperation Among Child Support, Medicaid, and SCHIP Agencies

Even though private health care coverage has advantages over public coverage — namely greater likelihood of full family coverage, a wider range of providers, no stigma, less taxpayer burden, and greater satisfaction with various aspects of care[33] — for the 8.5 million children who did not have any health insurance coverage in 2002, public health care coverage may need to be pursued if private health care coverage is not available or not accessible. There is general agreement that the CSE agency should work more closely with Medicaid/SCHIP to ensure that children who have access to private health care coverage obtain such coverage, and that those who are eligible for publicly-subsidized health coverage are covered by Medicaid or SCHIP.

Alternate Methods to Offset Health Insurance or Medicaid Costs

Although focused solely on the state of Connecticut, a 1998 report by the HHS Office of Inspector General (OIG) found many noncustodial parents who were required by court order to provide health care coverage to their children were unable to meet their obligation because either their employers did not offer health insurance or available health insurance was not reasonable in cost. One of the report's recommendations was for Connecticut to require noncustodial parents to pay all or part of the Medicaid premiums for their dependent children. The report estimated that Connecticut would save about $11.4 million annually in combined federal and state Medicaid costs if it required noncustodial parents to offset Medicaid premiums paid by the state on behalf of the children of these noncustodial parents.[34]

Similarly, a 2003 HHS OIG report focused on North Carolina found that about $17.4 million could have been collected from the noncustodial parents of 30,987 children to partially offset the Medicaid cost incurred by the state and federal governments to provide health care to these children.[35] Although federal law does not require noncustodial parents to provide medical support if the employer does not offer health insurance or the insurance is too costly, states have the authority to modify state laws to require noncustodial parents to contribute to their dependent children's Medicaid costs.

In cases where a parent has access to private health care coverage but it is too costly, the child may then be enrolled in Medicaid, if eligible. In such cases, it may be less expensive for the state if the child were enrolled in the private health care coverage. For example, the noncustodial parent's share of the private health insurance premium might be less than what the state pays an HMO for the child's

Medicaid coverage. In that case, many experts believe that it would make sense for Medicaid to pay the private health coverage premium.[36] Federal law allows individuals to obtain private health care coverage with a public subsidy. Specifically, section 1906 of the Social Security Act allows state Medicaid agencies to use Medicaid funds to purchase group health insurance coverage if such coverage is available to a Medicaid-eligible individual.

Closing the Gap Between Those Eligible for Medicaid and Those Enrolled

In many cases, children are uninsured because private health insurance coverage is not available through either parent, and the custodial parent has not enrolled the child in the available public health care system, i.e., Medicaid or SCHIP. One study estimates that enrolling uninsured, child support-eligible children in Medicaid or SCHIP could reduce the share of these children who are uninsured from 15% to 3%. According to some analysts, requiring that the child be enrolled in Medicaid or SCHIP (if eligible) when private coverage is not available should be a standard part of the child support process. Also, as mentioned above, consideration could also be given to having the noncustodial parent contribute to any premiums, co-payments, or deductibles associated with SCHIP coverage if the state in which the child is to be enrolled has a separate SCHIP program that imposes these costs. These types of procedures might spread the cost more equitably between the parents, and between parents and the state.[37]

If the state does not want to require enrollment in publicly-funded medical programs, it could provide information on the availability of the programs. It has been estimated that 66% of uninsured child support-eligible children are eligible for Medicaid, and another 15% are eligible for SCHIP. One of the main reasons for this lack of health care coverage of children who are eligible for public health care programs is that many parents do not know about Medicaid and SCHIP or do not know how to enroll their children. About one-third of the parents of eligible but not-enrolled children reported that they had not heard of Medicaid or SCHIP. Another 10% had difficulty with the enrollment process. An option would be for the CSE agency to provide parents with information about these programs and assist them in the enrollment process.[38]

The ability to move back and forth between the noncustodial parent's health insurance plan and an alternative source of coverage is an important factor in determining the best source of coverage for a child whose noncustodial parent has access to employment-based health care coverage on an irregular or seasonal basis. According to one author:

Transitions to and from Medicaid can be quite seamless, since children can remain enrolled in Medicaid even when they are also covered by the nonresident parent's health care plan (in which case, the nonresident parent's health care plan takes precedence). However, if the alternative source of coverage is SCHIP, then the transition may not be seamless, since some states require a child to be uninsured for three or more months before gaining eligibility. Unless some exemption can be made for children losing coverage from a nonresident parent, SCHIP-eligible children whose nonresident parent can provide only irregular access to employment-based health care coverage may be better off if some other form of medical support is required, such as a contribution to the health plan premiums paid by the custodial family, or contributions toward co-payments and deductibles.[39]

Legislative Timetables for Medical Support Have Not Been Met

P.L.105-200 provided for a uniform manner for states to inform employers about their need to enroll the children of noncustodial parents in employer-sponsored health plans. It required the CSE agency to use a standardized "National Medical Support Notice" (developed by HHS and the Department of Labor) to communicate to employers the issuance of a medical support order. Employers are required to accept the form as a "Qualified Medical Child Support Order" (QMCSO) under ERISA.[40] An appropriately completed national medical support notice is considered to be a QMCSO and as such must be honored by the employer's group health plan.

P.L. 105-200 also requires plans sponsored by churches and state and local governments to provide benefits in accordance with the requirements of an appropriately completed NMSN. The legislation envisioned that all states would be using the NMSN by October 1, 2001 or, at the latest, by the end of first legislative session to occur after that date, if state legislation was needed. It also required employers to honor any appropriately completed NMSN and send it to the appropriate plan administrator within 20 business days. The plan administrator has 40 days from the date on the NMSN to respond to the CSE agency. Finally, employers were required to notify the state CSE agency if the employee was terminated thereby alerting the CSE agency of the need to enforce medical support against any new employer by issuing another NMSN.

A draft NMSN was issued for public comment on November 15, 1999. Changes were made in response to comments from the Medical Child Support Working Group, as well as the public. The Department of Labor and the Department of Health and Human Services adopted final regulations on December

27, 2000, implementing the National Medical Support Notice provisions of the Child Support Performance and Incentive Act of 1998 (P.L. 105-200). On January 26, 2001, the Federal Register published a notice that delayed the effective date of the final NMSN regulations until March 27, 2001.

Although Congress required all state CSE agencies to use the NMSN once it was promulgated, few states had implemented it by the target date of October 2001. According to OCSE, 37 states and territories had to delay implementation of the NMSN because their legislatures needed to pass the required legislation. According to National Women's Law Center, as of September 2002, about 30 states had passed NMSN implementation legislation.[41] According to the Center on Law and Social Policy, as of April 4, 2003, about half the states were not yet using the NMSN.[42]

Federal law mandates that states have procedures under which all child support orders are required to include a provision for the health care coverage of the child (section 466(a)(19) of the Social Security Act). Federal law does not, however, stipulate state use of the NMSN in the CSE state plan requirements on provision of health care coverage.[43] Thus, a state that does not use the NMSN is not considered to be in noncompliance with the state CSE plan, and thereby is not subject to a financial penalty. Some observers contend that imposing financial sanctions on states that do not use the NMSN could increase its use and thereby increase enforcement of medical child support. Some states contend that the NMSN is much too long and cite the expense of mailing such a lengthy document to a large number of employers. Further, others note that federal law does not require that states impose financial penalties on employers who fail to comply with the NMSN (states, however, can impose such sanctions under state law). According to the National Women's Law Center, some states without relevant employer and plan administrator sanctions are concerned that the lack of sanctions may be an barrier to successful enforcement of medical child support.[44]

APPENDIX A: LEGISLATIVE HISTORY OF MEDICAL CHILD SUPPORT PROVISIONS

Just as Temporary Assistance for Needy Families (TANF) recipients must assign their child support rights to the state, so too must Medicaid recipients assign their medical support rights to the state. The impetus for the federal government moving into the arena of financial child support was to reduce federal expenditures on the old Aid to Families with Dependent Children (AFDC) entitlement program (which was replaced in 1996 by the time-limited TANF block grant program). Similarly, the impetus for the federal government moving into the arena of medical support for children (eligible for child support) was to reduce federal costs of the Medicaid program. This section of the report summarizes major medical child support provisions.

P.L. 95-142, Medicare-Medicaid Anti-Fraud and Abuse Amendments (H.R. 3), Enacted October 25, 1977

The first link between child support and medical support came as an attempt to recoup the costs of Medicaid provided to public assistance families under Title XIX of the Social Security Act. Just two years after the creation of the CSE (i.e., IV-D of the Social Security Act) program, the Medicare/Medicaid Anti-fraud and Abuse Amendments of 1977 established a medical support enforcement program that *allowed* states to require that Medicaid applicants assign their rights to medical support to the state. Further, in an effort to cover children with private insurance instead of public programs, when available, it permitted CSE and Medicaid agencies to enter into cooperative agreements to pursue medical child support assigned to the state. (It should be noted that activities performed by the CSE agency under a cooperative agreement with the Medicaid agency must be funded by the Medicaid agency.) The 1977 law also required state CSE agencies to notify Medicaid agencies when private family health coverage was either obtained or discontinued for a Medicaid-eligible person.

P.L. 98-369, the Deficit Reduction Act of 1984 (H.R. 4170), Enacted July 18, 1984

P.L. 98-369 *mandated* states to require that Medicaid applicants assign their rights to medical support to the state (Section 1912(a) of the Social Security Act).

P.L. 98-378, the Child Support Enforcement Amendments of 1984 (H.R. 4325), Enacted August 16, 1984

Section 16 of Public Law 98-378, enacted in 1984, required the HHS Secretary to issue regulations to require that state CSE agencies petition for the inclusion of medical support as part of any new or modified child support order whenever health care coverage is available at "reasonable cost" to the noncustodial parent of a child receiving AFDC, Medicaid, or foster care benefits or services. According to federal regulations, any employment-related or other group coverage was considered reasonable, under the assumption that health insurance is inexpensive to the employee/noncustodial parent.

Implementing Regulations
On October 16, 1985, the Office of Child Support Enforcement (OCSE) published regulations amending previous regulations and implementing section 16 of P. L. 98-378. The regulations required state CSE agencies to obtain basic medical support information and provide this information to the state Medicaid agency. The purpose of medical support enforcement is to expand the number of children for whom private health insurance coverage is obtained by increasing the availability of third party resources to pay for medical care, and thereby reduce Medicaid costs for both the states and the federal government. If the custodial parent does not have satisfactory health insurance coverage, the child support agency must petition the court or administrative authority to include medical support in new or modified support orders and inform the state Medicaid agency of any new or modified support orders that include a medical support obligation. The regulations also required CSE agencies to enforce medical support that has been ordered by a court or administrative process. States receive child support matching funds at the 66% rate for required medical support activities.

Before these 1985 regulations were issued, medical support activities were pursued by CSE agencies onlyunder optional cooperative agreements with Medicaid agencies. Some of the functions that the CSE agency may perform under a cooperative agreement with the Medicaid agency include: receiving referrals from the Medicaid agency, locating noncustodial parents, establishing paternity, determining whether the noncustodial parent has a health insurance policy or plan that covers the child, obtaining sufficient information about the health insurance policy or plan to permit the filing of a claim with the insurer, filing a claim with the insurer or transmitting the necessary information to the Medicaid agency, securing health insurance coverage through court or administrative order, and recovering amounts necessary to reimburse medical assistance payments.

More Regulations
On September 16, 1988, OCSE issued regulations expanding the medical support enforcement provisions. These regulations required the CSE agency to develop criteria to identify existing child support cases that have a high potential

for obtaining medical support, and to petition the court or administrative authorityto modifysupport orders to include medical support for these cases even if no other modification is anticipated. The CSE agency also is required to provide the custodial parent with information regarding the health insurance coverage obtained by the noncustodial parent for the child. Moreover, the regulation deleted the condition that CSE agencies may secure health insurance coverage under a cooperative agreement onlywhen it will not reduce the noncustodial parent's ability to pay child support.

P.L. 103-66, the Omnibus Budget Reconciliation Act of 1993 (H.R. 2264), Enacted August 10, 1993

Before late 1993, employees covered under their employers' health care plans generally could provide coverage to children only if the children lived with the employee. However, as a result of divorce proceedings, employees often lost custody of their children but were nonetheless required to provide their health care coverage. While the employee would be obliged to follow the court's directive, the employer that sponsored the employee's health care plan was under no similar obligation. Even if the court ordered the employer to continue health care coverage for the nonresident child of their employee, the employer would be under no legal obligation to do so.

Aware of this situation, Congress took the following legislative action in the Omnibus Budget Reconciliation Act of 1993 (P.L. 103-66):

1. Insurers were prohibited from denying enrollment of a child under the health insurance coverage of the child's parent on the grounds that the child was born out of wedlock, is not claimed as a dependent on the parent's federal income tax return, or does not reside with the parent or in the insurer's service area;

2. Insurers and employers were required, in any case in which a parent is required by court order to provide health coverage for a child and the child is otherwise eligible for family health coverage through the insurer: (a) to permit the parent, without regard to any enrollment season restrictions, to enroll the child under such family coverage; (b) if the parent fails to provide health insurance coverage for a child, to enroll the child upon application by the child's other parent or the state child support or Medicaid agency; and (c) with respect to employers, not to disenroll the child unless there is satisfactory written evidence that the

order is no longer in effect or the child is or will be enrolled in comparable health coverage through another insurer that will take effect not later than the effective date of the disenrollment;

3. Employers doing business in the state, if they offer health insurance and if a court order is in effect, were required to withhold from the employee's compensation the employee's share of premiums for health insurance and to pay that share to the insurer. The HHS Secretary may provide by regulation for such exceptions to this requirement (and other requirements described above that apply to employers) as the Secretary determines necessaryto ensure compliance with an order, or with the limits on withholding that are specified in section 303(b) of the Consumer Credit Protection Act;

4. Insurers were prohibited from imposing requirements on a state agency acting as an agent or assignee of an individual eligible for medical assistance that are different from requirements applicable to an agent or assignee of any other individual;

5. Insurers were required, in the case of a child who has coverage through the insurer of a noncustodial parent to: (a) provide the custodial parent with the information necessary for the child to obtain benefits; (b) permit the custodial parent (or provider, with the custodial parent's approval) to submit claims for covered services without the approval of the noncustodial parent; and (c) make payment on claims directly to the custodial parent, the provider, or the state agency; and

6. The state Medicaid agency was permitted to garnish the wages, salary, or other employment income of, and to withhold state tax refunds to, any person who: (a) is required by court or administrative order to provide health insurance coverage to an individual eligible for Medicaid; (b) has received payment from a third party for the costs of medical services to that individual; and (c) has not reimbursed either the individual or the provider. The amount subject to garnishment or withholding is the amount required to reimburse the state agency for expenditures for costs of medical services provided under the Medicaid program. Claims for current or past due child support take priority over any claims for the costs of medical services.

P.L. 104-193, the Personal Responsibility and Work Opportunity Reconciliation Act of 1996 (H.R. 3734), Enacted August 22, 1996

Under the 1996 welfare reform legislation, the definition of "medical child support order" in the Employee Retirement Income Security Act (ERISA) was expanded to clarify that any judgment, decree, or order that is issued by a court or by an administrative process has the force and effect of law. In addition, the 1996 welfare reform law stipulated that all orders enforced by the state CSE agency must include a provision for health care coverage. If the noncustodial parent changes jobs and the new employer provides health coverage, the state must send notice of coverage to the new employer; the notice must serve to enroll the child in the health plan of the new employer. (Before enactment of P.L. 104-193, families who were not receiving public assistance benefits could choose not to seek medical support.)

P.L. 105-200, the Child Support Performance and Incentive Act of 1998 (H.R. 3130), Enacted July 16, 1998

P.L.105-200 provided for a uniform manner for states to inform employers about their need to enroll the children of noncustodial parents in employer-sponsored health plans. It required the CSE agency to use a standardized "National Medical Support Notice" (developed by HHS and the Department of Labor) to communicate to employers the issuance of a medical support order. Employers are required to accept the form as a "Qualified Medical Support Order" under ERISA. States were required to begin using the national medical support notice in October 2001, although many states had to delay implementation until enactment of required state enabling legislation. An appropriately completed national medical support notice is considered to be a "Qualified Medical Child Support Order" and as such must be honored by the employer's group health plan.

P.L. 105-200 also called for the joint establishment of a Medical Support Working Group by the Secretaries of HHS and Labor to identify impediments to the effective enforcement of medical support by state CSE agencies and to submit to the Secretaries of HHS and Labor a report containing recommendations addressing the identified impediments.

In addition, the HHS Secretary, in consultation with state CSE directors and representatives of children potentially eligible for medical support, was directed to develop a performance measure based on the effectiveness of states in establishing and enforcing medical support obligations and to make recommendations for the incorporation of the measure in a revenue neutral manner into the Child Support Incentive Payment System, no later than October 1, 1999.

APPENDIX B: HEALTH CARE COVERAGE OF CUSTODIAL CHILDREN — 1993

Table B.1. Provision for Health Care Costs in the Child Support Award or Agreement, 1993

	Custodial family income level		
	<200% Poverty	200% Poverty+	Total
Families with a Formal Child Support Award or Agreement	2,858	2,244	5,102
Noncustodial father to provide health care coverage	37%	38%	37%
Custodial family to provide health care coverage	11%	21%	16%
Other provision for health care costs	9%	9%	9%
No provision for health care costs	43%	32%	38%

Source: LauraWheaton, The Urban Institute, *Nonresident Fathers: To What Extent Do They Have Access to Employment-Based Health Care Coverage?*, June 2000, p. 6 of web version [http://fatherhood.hhs.gov/ncp-health00/report.htm].

Table B.2. Health Care Coverage of Children in Custodial Families in 1993

	Custodial family income level		
	<200% Poverty	200% Poverty+	Total
All custodial families (thousands)	6,636	3,591	10,227
Health care coverage provided by:*	(100%)	(100%)	100%
Noncustodial father	21%	30%	24%
Custodial parent	21%	61%	35%
Medicaid/Medicare only	50%	5%	35%
Uninsured	8%	4%	6%
With private coverage entire year	23%	79%	43%
Custodial families where noncustodial father required to provide health care coverage (thousands)	1,062	846	1,908
Health care coverage provided by:*	(100%)	(100%)	(100%)
Noncustodial father	66%	71%	68%

Table B.2. Continued

	Custodial family income level		
	<200% Poverty	200% Poverty+	Total
Custodial parent	12%	24%	17%
Medicaid/Medicare only	18%	2%	11%
Uninsured	4%	3%	4%
With private coverage entire year	48%	87%	65%
Custodial families with award or agreement, but father not required to provide health care coverage (thousands)	1,795	1,398	3,193
Health care coverage provided by:*	(100%)	(100%)	(100%)
Noncustodial father	15%	16%	15%
Custodial parent	26%	77%	49%
Medicaid/Medicare only	52%	3%	30%
Uninsured	7%	4%	6%
With private coverage entire year	22%	83%	49%
No award or agreement (thousands)	3,779	1,346	5,125
Health care coverage provided by:*	(100%)	(100%)	(100%)
Noncustodial father	10%	18%	12%
Custodial parent	21%	68%	33%
Medicaid/Medicare only	59%	10%	46%
Uninsured	10%	4%	8%
With private coverage entire year	16%	69%	30%

Source: Laura Wheaton, The Urban Institute, *Nonresident Fathers: To What Extent Do They Have Access to Employment-Based Health Care Coverage?*, June 2000, p. 7 and 8 of web version [http://fatherhood.hhs.gov/ncp-health00/report.htm].

* If at least one custodial child receives health care coverage from a given source in at lest one month of the year, then the family is considered to have received health care coverage from that source. The family is placed into the first of the categories that applies to it.

REFERENCES

[1]   CSE agency staff carry out this duty by determining the employment status of the noncustodial parent and whether health insurance coverage is available for his or her dependents. If such coverage is available, the CSE agency notifies the employer of the employee's medical child support obligation and the employer's responsibility to thereby enroll the dependents of the employee in the health care plan.

[2] For background information on the CSE program, see: Congressional Research Service (CRS) Report 97-408, Child Support Enforcement: New Reforms and Potential Issues, by Carmen Solomon-Fears.

[3] U.S. Department of Health and Human Services, Administration for Children and Families, Office of Child Support Enforcement, *Essentials for Attorneys in Child Support Enforcement, 3rd Edition*, 2002 at [http://www.acf.hhs.gov/programs/cse/pubs/2002/reports/essentials/index.html].

[4] U.S. Department of Health and Human Services, Administration for Children and Families, Office of Child Support Enforcement, OCSE-AT-88-15, Action Transmittal, *Medical Support Enforcement*, Sept. 26, 1988.

[5] Generally, a state court or agency may require an ERISA-covered health plan to provide health benefits coverage to children by issuing a Qualified Medical Child Support Order; the medical support order is *"qualified"* if it includes the information mentioned above. The National Medical Support Notice is a federally-required form that serves the same purpose as the QMCSO. The standardized form was designed in consultation with a federal workgroup that included representatives of major employers, payroll associations, insurance administrators and government representatives. Their intent was to provide employers with a standardized set of forms, processes and timeframes — something employers had requested.

[6] In FY2001, medical support payments to families amounted to $94.3 million, up from $32.3 million in FY1994 (and $7.5 million in FY1993, the first year in which data were collected).

[7] U.S. Department of Health and Human Services, Administration for Children and Families, Office of Child Support Enforcement, *Essentials for Attorneys in Child Support Enforcement, 3rd Edition*, 1992, p. 109.

[8] U.S. Congress, Conference Committees, *Child Support Enforcement Amendments of 1984*, conference report to accompany H.R. 4325, 98th Cong., 2nd sess., H.Rept. 98-925 (Washington, GPO, 1984), p. 52-53.

[9] U.S. Department of Labor, Pension and Welfare Benefits Administration, *Federal Register*, v. 65, no. 249, National Medical Support Notice, Dec. 27, 2000, p. 82137.

[10] The 1991 Survey was the first survey to include information on custodial fathers.

[11] Laura Wheaton, The Urban Institute, Prepared for Office of the Assistant Secretary for Planning and Evaluation, U.S. Department of Health and Human Services, Contract No. HHS-100-95-0021, *Nonresident Fathers: To What Extent Do They Have Access to Employment-Based Health Care*

Coverage?, June 2000, p. 18 of web version [http://fatherhood.hhs.gov/ncp-health00/report.htm]. (Hereafter cited as *Nonresident Fathers*.)

[12] U.S. Department of Health and Human Services, Office of Inspector General, *Medical Insurance for Dependents Receiving Child Support*, OEI-07-97-00500, June 2000, p. 2.

[13] U.S. Department of Health and Human Services, Administration for Children and Families, Office of Child Support Enforcement, *21 Million Children's Health: Our Shared Responsibility — The Medical Child Support Working Group's Report*, June 2000, p. 2-10. (Hereafter cited as *21 Million Children's Health*.)

[14] The Medical Child Support Working Group, congressionally-mandated by P.L. 105-200, included 30 members representing HHS and the Department of Labor (DOL), state CSE directors, state Medicaid directors, employers (including small business owners and payroll professionals), sponsors and administrators of group health plans, organizations representing children potentially eligible for medical support, state medical child support programs, and organizations representing state CSE programs.

[15] Paula Roberts, Center for Law and Social Policy, *Improving Health Care Coverage in the Child Support System*, Apr. 1997, p. 11-14. See also Anne R. Gordon, Urban Institute Press, Child Support and Child Well-Being, Chapter 3, *Implementation of the Income Withholding and Medical Support Provisions of the 1984 Child Support Enforcement Amendments*, p. 61-92.

[16] The Federal Consumer Credit Protection Act (Title 15 USC Sec. 1673) limits garnishment to 50% of disposable earnings for a noncustodial parent who is the head of a household, and 60% for a noncustodial parent who is not supporting a second family. These percentages increase by 5 percentage points, to 55% and 65% respectively, when the arrearages represent support that was due more than 12 weeks before the current pay period.

[17] Paula Roberts, Center for Law and Social Policy, *Failure to Thrive: The Continuing Poor Health of Medical Child Support*, June 2003, p. 5-6. (Hereafter cited as *Failure to Thrive*.)

[18] Daniel R. Meyer, University of Wisconsin, Madison, Institute for Research on Poverty, *Health Insurance and Child Support*, Discussion Paper, DP#1042-94, Sept. 1994, p. 5.

[19] *21 Million Children's Health*, p. 2-19.

[20] Noncustodial parents enrolled in other managed care arrangements, such as a Preferred Provider Organization (PPO) or Point of Service (POS), should be able to extend coverage to children living elsewhere, since these plans allow the use of out-of-network medical providers. But, reliance on out-of-

network medical providers usually results in higher out-of-pocket costs and/or restricted benefits.

[21] *Failure to Thrive*, p. 8.

[22] *21 Million Children's Health*, p. 2-19.

[23] Ibid., p. 3-10.

[24] *Nonresident Fathers*, p. 11-12.

[25] The federal government provides 90% matching funds for laboratory costs incurred in determining paternity. In addition, for many years the federal government also reimbursed state costs of designing and implementing automated data processing and information retrieval systems at a 90% match rate. During the period FY1996-FY2001, the federal matching rate was reduced to 80% of a capped amount. Beginning October 1, 2001 (i.e., FY2002), the federal matching rate for CSE computerization was reduced back to 66%.

[26] U.S. Congress, House Committee on Ways and Means, *Child Support Performance and Incentive Act of 1998*, report to accompany H.R. 3130, 105th Cong., 2nd sess., H.Rept. 105-422 (Washington: GPO, 1998), p. 35.

[27] In the report to Congress, the group was called the Medical Support Indicator Work Group. The Group met on June 2, 1998 and again on March 2-3,1999. The HHS Secretary submitted the required report to Congress on June 23, 1999.

[28] Ibid., p. 3-10 — 3-15.

[29] Ibid., p. 3-11 — 3-15.

[30] Ibid., p. 2-19.

[31] U.S. Department of Health and Human Services, Administration for Children and Families, Office of Child Support Enforcement, Policy Interpretation Questions, PIQ-03-08, *Medical Support in Child Support Orders-Definition of Reasonable Cost*, July 25, 2003.

[32] *21 Million Children's Health*, p. 3-11 — 3-15.

[33] Amy J. Davidoff, Bowen Garrett, Diane M. Makuc, and Matthew Schirmer, The Urban Institute, *Children Eligible for Medicaid but Not Enrolled: How Great a Policy Concern?*, series A, no. A-41, Sept. 2000, p. 6.

[34] U.S. Department of Health and Human Services, Office of Inspector General, *Review of Availability of Health Insurance for Title IV-D Children*, A-O 1-97-02506, June 1998.

[35] U.S. Department of Health and Human Services, Office of Inspector General, *Review To Increase the Number of Noncustodial Parents Providing Medical Support to Their Children and Reduce Medicaid Costs in North Carolina*, A-04-02-00013, June 2003.

[36] *Failure to Thrive*, p. 20.

[37] Ibid., p. 17.

[38] Ibid., p. 17-20.

[39] *Nonresident Fathers*, p. 16-17.

[40] At the same time that the QMCSO provisions were added to ERISA, Congress also added section 1908 (later changed to section 1908A) to the Social Security Act. Section 1908A of the SSA conditions state eligibility for Medicaid matching funds on the enactment of certain specified state laws relating to medical child support. Under section 1908A states must enact laws under which insurers (including group health plans) may not deny enrollment of a child under the health coverage of the child's parent on the ground that the child is born out of wedlock, not claimed as a dependent on the parent's tax return, or not in residence with the parent or in the insurer's service area. Section 1908 also sets out rules for states to require of employers and insurers when a parent is ordered by a court or administrative agency to provide health coverage for a child and the parent is eligible for health coverage from that insurer or employer, including a provision which permits the custodial parent or the state CSE agency to apply for available coverage for the child, without regard to open season restrictions. Source: *Federal Register*, v. 65, no. 249, Dec. 27, 2000, p. 82128.

[41] National Women's Law Center, *Implementing the National Medical Support Notice: Insights From State Experiences*, Sept. 2002. (Hereafter cited as *Implementing the National Medical Support Notice*.)

[42] *Failure to Thrive*, p. 14-15.

[43] P.L. 104-193, the 1996 welfare reform law made revisions to section 466(a)(19) of the Social Security Act, including the elimination of the *general* reference to the National Medical Support Notice. Federal law does provide that "in the case in which a noncustodial parent provides such [health care] coverage and changes employment, and the new employer provides health care coverage, the State agency shall transfer notice of the provision to the employer, which notice shall operate to enroll the child in the noncustodial parent's health plan, unless the noncustodial parent contests the notice."

[44] *Implementing the National Medical Support Notice*, p. 2-3.

In: Family Structure and Support Issues
Editor: A. E. Bennett, pp. 65-74

ISBN: 1-60021-340-5
© 2007 Nova Science Publishers, Inc.

Chapter 4

CHILD SUPPORT ENFORCEMENT: PROGRAM BASICS*

Carmen Solomon-Fears

ABSTRACT

The Child Support Enforcement (CSE) program was enacted in 1975 as a federal-state program (Title IV-D of the Social Security Act) to help strengthen families by securing financial support for children from their noncustodial parent on a consistent and continuing basis and by helping some families to remain self-sufficient and off public assistance by providing the requisite CSE services. Over the years, CSE has evolved into a multifaceted program. While cost-recovery still remains an important function of the program, its other aspects include service delivery and promotion of self-sufficiency and parental responsibility. In FY2004, the CSE program collected $21.9 billion in child support payments and served 15.9 million child support cases. However, the program still collects only 18% of child support obligations for which it has responsibility and collects payments for only 51% of its caseload.

---

* Excerpted from CRS Report RS22380, dated February 15, 2006.

BACKGROUND

The CSE program, Part D of Title IV of the Social Security Act, was enacted in January 1975 (P.L. 93-647). The CSE program is administered by the Office of Child Support Enforcement (OCSE) in the Department of Health and Human Services (HHS), and funded by general revenues. All 50 states, the District of Columbia, Guam, Puerto Rico, and the Virgin Islands operate CSE programs and are entitled to federal matching funds.[1] Families receiving Temporary Assistance to Needy Families (TANF) benefits (Title IV-A), foster care payments, or Medicaid coverage automatically qualify for CSE services free of charge. Other families must apply for CSE services, and states must charge an application fee that cannot exceed $25.[2] Child support collected on behalf of nonwelfare families goes to the family, usually through the state disbursement unit.

Child Support Data — FY2004 (Preliminary)

Total CSE caseload	*Total*, 15.9 million; *TANF*, 2.6 million; *former-TANF*, 7.3 million; *never-TANF*, 5.9 million
Total CSE collections	*Total*, $21.861 billion; *TANF* families, $1.105 billion (plus $1.9 billion on behalf of Medicaid-only families); *former-TANF*, $9.359 billion; *never-TANF*, $9.505 billion
Payments to families	*Total*, $19.7 billion; *TANF*, $179 million (plus $1.9 billion on behalf of Medicaid-only families); *former-TANF*, $8.1 billion; *never*-TANF, $9.5 billion
Federal share of TANF collections	$1.147 billion
State share of TANF collections	$927 million
Medical support payments	$111 million
Total CSE expenditures	$5.322 billion; *federal share*, $3.519 billion, *state share*, $1.803 billion
Incentive payments to states	$361 million (estimate); maximum statutory amount $454 million
Paternities established and acknowledged	1,606,303
Support orders established	1,181,012 (includes only new orders; excludes modifications)
Collections made	For 8,133,646 *total* families; *TANF* families, 781,188; *former-TANF* families, 3,852,255; *never-TANF* families, 3,500,203

Source: Table prepared by the Congressional Research Service, based on data from the Office of Child Support Enforcement, Department of Health and Human Services.
Note: Some totals are imprecise because of rounding.

Collections on behalf of families receiving cash TANF block grant benefits are used to reimburse state and federal governments for TANF payments made to the family.

Between FY1978 and FY2004, child support payments collected by CSE agencies increased from $1 billion in FY1978 to $21.9 billion in FY2004, and the number of children whose paternity was established or acknowledged increased from 111,000 to 1.606 million. However, the program still collects only 18% of child support obligations for which it has responsibility[3] and collects payments for only 51% of its caseload. OCSE data indicate that in FY2004, paternity had been established or acknowledged for about 80% of the 10 million children on the CSE caseload without legally identified fathers. The CSE program is estimated to handle at least 50% of all child support cases; the remaining cases are handled by private attorneys, collection agencies, or through mutual agreements between the parents.

PROGRAM ELEMENTS

The CSE program provides seven major services on behalf of children: (1) parent location, (2) paternity establishment, (3) establishment of child support orders, (4) review and modification of support orders, (5) collection of support payments, (6) distribution of support payments, and (7) establishment and enforcement of medical support.[4]

Locating Absent Parents

To improve the CSE agency's ability to locate absent parents, states are required to have automated registries of child support orders that contain records of each case in which CSE services are being provided and all new or modified child support orders. The state registry includes a record of the support owed under the order, arrearages, interest or late penalty charges, amounts collected, amounts distributed, the child's date of birth, and any liens imposed; and also includes standardized information on both parents, such as name, Social Security number, date of birth, and case identification number. States also must establish an automated directory of new hires containing information from employers, including federal, state, and local governments and labor organizations, for each newly hired employee, that includes the name, address and Social Security number of the employee and the employer's name, address, and tax identification number. This information generally is supplied to the state new hires directory within 20 days after the employee is hired. Moreover, federal law required the establishment of a federal case registry of child support orders and a national directory of new hires.[5] The federal directories consist of information from the state directories and federal agencies, and are located in the Federal Parent Locator Service (FPLS).

Federal law allows all states to link up to an array of databases, and permits the FPLS to be used for the purpose of establishing parentage; establishing, setting the amount of, modifying, or enforcing child support obligations; and enforcing child custody or visitation orders.[6] Federal law requires that a designated state agency, directly or by contract, conduct automated comparisons of the Social Security numbers reported by employers to the state directory of new hires and the Social Security numbers of CSE cases that appear in the records of the state registry of child support orders. Federal law requires the HHS Secretary to conduct similar comparisons of the federal directories.[7] Automation is critical to the operation and success of the CSE program.[8]

Paternity Establishment

Legally identifying the father is a prerequisite for obtaining a child support order. Under federal law TANF block grant applicants and recipients are required to cooperate in establishing paternity or obtaining support payments. Moreover, a penalty for noncooperation exists — if it is determined that an individual is not cooperating and the individual does not qualify for any good cause or other exception, then the state must reduce the family's TANF benefit by at least 25% and may remove the family from the TANF program. Federal law also (1) requires that paternity be established for 90% of the CSE cases needing such a determination, (2) requires a simple civil process for establishing paternity, (3) requires a uniform affidavit to be completed by men voluntarily acknowledging paternity and entitles the affidavit to full faith and credit in any state, (4) stipulates that a signed acknowledgment of paternity be considered a legal finding of paternity unless it is rescinded within 60 days, and thereafter may be challenged in court only on the basis of fraud, duress, or material mistake of fact, (5) provides that no judicial or administrative action is needed to ratify an acknowledgment that is not challenged, and (6) requires all parties to submit to genetic testing in contested paternity cases. (See CRS Report RL31467, *Paternity Establishment: Child Support and Beyond,* by Carmen Solomon-Fears.)

Establishment of Child Support Orders

A child support order legally obligates noncustodial parents to provide financial support for their children and stipulates the amount of the obligation (current monthly obligation plus arrearages, if any) and how it is to be paid. A child support order is usually established at the time of divorce or when a welfare case is initiated. The 1988 child support amendments (P.L. 100-485) required states to use their state-established guidelines in establishing child support orders. States decide child support amounts based on the noncustodial parent's income or based on both parents' income; other factors include the age of child, whether a stepparent is in the home, whether the child is disabled, and the number of siblings.

Review and Modification of Support Orders

Without periodic modifications, child support obligations can become inadequate or inequitable. Under current law, states generally must review child support orders every three years to determine if the order should be adjusted to reflect the parent's financial circumstances.[9]

Enforcement

Collection methods used by state CSE agencies include income withholding,[10] intercept of federal and state income tax refunds, intercept of unemployment compensation, liens against property, reporting child support obligations to credit bureaus, intercept of lottery winnings, sending insurance settlement information to CSE agencies, authority to withhold or suspend driver's licenses, professional licenses, and recreational and sporting licenses of persons who owe past-due support, and authority to seize assets of debtor parents held by public or private retirement funds and financial institutions. Moreover, federal law authorizes the Secretary of State to deny, revoke, or restrict passports of debtor parents. All jurisdictions also have civil or criminal contempt-of-court procedures and criminal nonsupport laws. In addition, federal criminal penalties may be imposed in certain cases. Federal law also requires states to enact and implement the Uniform Interstate Family Support Act (UIFSA), and expand full faith and credit procedures. Federal law also provides for international enforcement of child support.[11]

Financing

The federal government reimburses each state 66% of the cost of operating its CSE program. However, it reimburses states at a higher 90% matching rate for the laboratory costs of establishing paternity.[12] In addition, the federal government pays states an incentive payment to encourage them to operate effective programs.[13] Federal law requires states to reinvest CSE incentive payments back into the CSE program or related activities.[14]

Collection and Disbursement

All states are required to have a centralized automated state collection and disbursement unit to which child support payments are paid and from which they are distributed. Federal law generally requires employers to remit to the state disbursement unit (SDU) income withheld within seven business days after the employee's payday. Further, the SDU is required to send child support payments to custodial parents within two business days of receipt of such payments.

Distribution of Support

Distribution rules determine which claim is paid first when a child support collection occurs. The order of payment of the child support collection is important because in many cases arrearages are never fully paid. While the family receives TANF cash benefits, the states and federal government retain any current support and any assigned arrearages collected up to the cumulative amount of TANF benefits paid to the family. While states may pay their share of collections to the family, they must pay the federal government the federal government's share of child support collections collected on behalf of TANF families. This means that the state, and not the federal government, bears the entire cost of any child support passed through to families (and disregarded by the state in determining the family's TANF cash benefit).[15]

States must distribute to former TANF families the following child support collections first before the state and the federal government are reimbursed (the "family-first" policy): (1) all current child support, (2) any child support arrearages that accrue after the family leaves TANF (these arrearages are called never-assigned arrearages), plus (3) any arrearages that accrued before the family began receiving TANF benefits. An exception to this rule occurs when child support arrearages are collected via the federal income tax refund offset program — those collections are divided between the state and federal government.[16] (Any child support arrearages that accrue during the time the family is on TANF belong to the state and federal government.)

VISITATION GRANTS AND RESPONSIBLE FATHERHOOD INITIATIVES

Historically, Congress has agreed that visitation and child support should be legally separate issues, and that only child support should be under the purview of the CSE program. Both federal and state policymakers have maintained that denial of visitation rights should be treated separately, and should not be considered a reason for stopping child support payments. However, in recognition of the negative long-term consequences for children associated with the absence of their father P.L. 104-193 (enacted in 1996) provided $10 million per year for grants to states for access and visitation programs, including mediation, counseling, education, and supervised visitation. P.L. 109-171 (enacted February 8, 2006) provides $50 million per year for five years in competitive grants for responsible fatherhood initiatives to states, territories, Indian tribes and tribal organizations, and public and nonprofit organizations, including religious organizations.

REFERENCES

[1]   States were historically required to provide CSE services to Indian tribes and tribal organizations as part of the CSE caseloads. The 1996 welfare reform law (P.L. 104-193) allowed direct federal funding of tribal CSE programs at a 90% federal matching rate. Currently, nine Indian Tribes or tribal organizations operate CSE programs. They are the Chickasaw Nation, Navajo Nation, Puyallup Tribe, Sisseton-Wahpeton Sioux Tribe, Lac du Flambeau Tribe, Menominee Tribe, Port Gamble S'Klallam, Lummi Nation, and the Forest County Potawatomi.

[2]   P.L. 109-171, effective October 1, 2006, requires families that have never been on TANF to pay a $25 annual user fee when child support enforcement efforts on their behalf are successful (i.e., at least $500 annually is collected on their behalf).

[3]   In FY2004, $130.3 billion in child support obligations ($28.0 billion in
       current support and $102.4 billion in past-due support) was owed to families
       receiving CSE services, but only $23.2 billion was paid ($16.5 billion
       current, $6.7 billion past-due).

[4]   Medical child support can take several forms. A noncustodial parent may be
       ordered to provide health insurance if available through his or her employer,
       pay for private health insurance premiums, or reimburse the custodial parent
       for all or a portion of the costs of health insurance obtained by the custodial
       parent. Federal law requires every child support order to include a provision
       for health care coverage. States are required to include provisions for health
       care coverage in their child support guidelines, and the CSE program is
       required to pursue private health care coverage when such coverage is
       available through a noncustodial parent's employer at a reasonable cost.
       P.L. 109-171 requires that medical support for a child be provided by either
       or both parents and that it must be enforced. It authorizes the state CSE
       agency to enforce medical support against a custodial parent whenever
       health care coverage is available to the custodial parent at reasonable cost.
       Moreover, it stipulates that medical support may include health care
       coverage (including payment of costs of premiums, co-payments, and
       deductibles) and payment of medical expenses incurred on behalf of a child.

[5]   Within three business days after receipt of new hire information from the
       employer, the state directory of new hires is required to furnish the
       information to the national directory of new hires.

[6]   P.L. 104-193 permitted both custodial and certain noncustodial parents to
       obtain information from the FPLS. P.L. 105-33, however, prohibited FPLS
       information from being disclosed to noncustodial parents in cases where
       there is evidence of domestic violence or child abuse, and the local court
       determines that disclosure may result in harm to the custodial parent or
       child.

[7]   When a match occurs, the state directory of new hires is required to report
       to the state CSE agency the name, date of birth, Social Security number of
       the employee, and the employer's name, address, and identification number.
       Within two business days, the CSE agency then instructs appropriate
       employers to withhold child support obligations from the employee's
       paycheck, unless the employee's income is not subject to income
       withholding.

[8]   Federal CSE law requires suspension of all federal CSE payments to the
       state when its CSE plan, after appeal, is disapproved. Moreover, states
       without approved CSE plans could lose funding for the TANF block grant.

P.L. 105-200 imposed substantially smaller financial penalties on states that failed to meet the automated data systems requirements. The HHS Secretary is required to reduce the amount the state would otherwise have received in federal child support funding by the penalty amount for the fiscal year in question. The penalty amount percentage is 4% in the case of the first year of noncompliance (FY1998); 8% in the second year (FY1999); 16% in the third year (FY2000); 25% in the fourth year (FY2001); and 30% in the fifth or any subsequent year.

[9] If a noncustodial parent cannot pay his or her child support payments because of unemployment, imprisonment, etc., then the noncustodial parent must immediately contact the court in order to have the child support order modified. Pursuant to federal law, the court will not be able to retroactively reduce the back payments (i.e., arrearages) that the noncustodial parent owes.

[10] There are three exceptions to the immediate income withholding rule: (1) if one of the parties demonstrates, and the court (or administrative process) finds that there is good cause not to require immediate withholding, (2) if both parties agree in writing to an alternative arrangement, or (3) at the HHS Secretary's discretion, if a state can demonstrate that the rule will not increase the effectiveness or efficiency of the state's CSE program.

[11] The CSE program has reciprocating agreements regarding the enforcement of child support with 10 countries: Australia, Canada, Czech Republic, Ireland, Netherlands, Norway, Poland, Portugal, Slovak Republic, and Switzerland.

[12] P.L. 109-171 stipulates that the 90% federal matching rate for laboratory costs associated with paternity establishment is to be reduced to 66% beginning October 1, 2006.

[13] The CSE incentive payment — which is based in part on five performance measures related to establishment of paternity and child support orders, collection of current and past-due child support payments, and cost-effectiveness — was statutorily set by P.L. 105-200. In the aggregate, incentive payments to states may not exceed $458 million for FY2006, $471 million for FY2007, and $483 million for FY2008 (to be increased for inflation in years thereafter).

[14] P.L. 109-171, effective October 1, 2007, prohibits federal matching of state expenditure of federal CSE incentive payments. This means that CSE incentive payments that are received by states and reinvested in the CSE program are not eligible for federal reimbursement.

[15] P.L. 109-171 helps states pay for the cost of their CSE pass-through and disregard policies by requiring the federal government to share in the costs of the entire amount of child support collections passed through and disregarded by states.

[16] P.L. 109-171 gives states the option of distributing to former TANF families the full amount of child support collected on their behalf (i.e., both current support and all child support arrearages — including arrearages collected through the federal income tax refund offset program).

In: Family Structure and Support Issues   ISBN: 1-60021-340-5
Editor: A. E. Bennett, pp. 75-84   © 2007 Nova Science Publishers, Inc.

Chapter 5

CHILD SUPPORT ENFORCEMENT: NEW REFORMS AND POTENTIAL ISSUES*

Carmen Solomon-Fears

ABSTRACT

P.L. 104-193 (the 1996 welfare reform legislation) made major changes to the Child Support Enforcement (CSE) program. Some of the changes include requiring states to increase the percentage of fathers identified, establishing an integrated, automated network linking all states to information about the location and assets of parents, and requiring states to implement more enforcement techniques to obtain collections from debtor parents. Additional legislative changes were made in 1997, 1998, and 1999, but not in 2000, 2001, or 2002. This chapter describes several aspects of the revised CSE program and discusses three issues that probably will be reexamined by the 108th Congress — CSE financing, parental access by noncustodial parents, and distribution of support payments.

---

* Excerpted from CRS Report 97-408 EPW, dated June 30, 2003.

BACKGROUND

The CSE program, Part D of Title IV of the Social Security Act, was enacted in January 1975 (P.L. 93-647). The CSE program is administered by the Office of Child Support Enforcement (OCSE) in the Department of Health and Human Services (HHS), and funded by general revenues. All 50 states, the District of Columbia, Guam, Puerto Rico, and the Virgin Islands operate CSE programs and are entitled to federal matching funds. The following families automatically qualify for CSE services (free of charge): families receiving (or who formerly received) Temporary Assistance to Needy Families (TANF) benefits (Title IV-A), foster care payments, or Medicaid coverage. Other families must apply for CSE services, and states must charge an application fee that cannot exceed $25.

Child Support Data — FY2002
(caseload numbers are unduplicated)

Total CSE caseload	*Total*, 16.1 million; *TANF*, 2.8 million; *former-TANF*, 7.4 million; *never-TANF*, 5.9 million
Total CSE collections	*Total*, $20.137 billion; *TANF* families, $1.682 billion; *former-TANF*, $8.298 billion; *never-TANF*, $10.156 billion
Payments to families	*Total*, $17.9 billion; *TANF*, $737 million; *former-TANF*, $7.0 billion; *never-TANF*, $10.1 billion
Federal share of TANF collections (net),	$ 1,180 million
State share of TANF collections,	$ 950 million
Incentive payments to States,	$338 million (estimate)
Medical support payments,	$89 million
Total CSE expenditures	$5.183 billion *federal share*, $3.432 billion, *state share*, $1.752 billion
Paternities established and acknowledged	1,517,897
Support orders established	1,220,078 (only includes new orders, excludes modifications)
Collections made	for 7,820,254 *total* families; *TANF* families, 805,983; *former-TANF* families, 3,769,703; *never-TANF* families, 3,244,568

Child support collected on behalf of nonwelfare families goes to the family (usually through the state disbursement unit). Collections on behalf of families receiving TANF benefits are used to reimburse state and federal governments for TANF payments made to the family.

Between FY1978 and FY2002, child support payments collected by CSE agencies increased from $1 billion in FY1978 to $20.1 billion in FY2002, and the number of children whose paternity was established (or acknowledged) increased by 1,268%, from 111,000 to 1.518 million. However, the program still collects only 18% of child support obligations for which it has responsibility[1] and collects payments for only 49% of its caseload. Moreover, OCSE data indicate that in FY2002, paternity had been established or acknowledged for only about 74% of the nearly 10.1 million children on the CSE caseload without legally identified fathers. The CSE program is estimated to handle at least 50% of all child support cases; the remaining cases are handled by private attorneys, collection agencies, or through mutual agreements between the parents.

PROGRAM ELEMENTS

The CSE program provides seven major services on behalf of children: (1) parent location, (2) paternity establishment, (3) establishment of child support orders, (4) review and modification of support orders, (5) collection of support payments, (6) distribution of support payments, and (7) establishment and enforcement of medical support.

Locating Absent Parents

To improve the CSE agency's ability to locate absent parents, P.L. 104-193 required states to have automated registries of child support orders, beginning October 1, 1998, containing records of each case in which CSE services are being provided and all new or modified child support orders. The state registry includes a record of the support owed under the order, arrearages, interest or late penalty charges, amounts collected, amounts distributed, child's date of birth, and any liens imposed; and also includes standardized information on both parents, such as name, Social Security number, date of birth, and case identification number. P.L. 104-193 required states, beginning October 1, 1997, to establish an automated directory of new hires containing information from employers, including federal, state, and local governments and labor organizations, for each newly hired employee, that includes the name, address and Social Securitynumber of the employee and the employer's name, address, and tax identification number.

This information generally is supplied to the state new hires directory within 20 days after the employee is hired. P.L. 104-193 also required the establishment of a federal case registry of child support orders and a national directory of new hires.[2] The federal directories consists of information from the state directories and is located in the Federal Parent Locator Service (FPLS).

P.L. 104-193 allowed all states to link up to an array of data bases and permits the FPLS to be used for the purpose of establishing parentage; establishing, setting the amount of, modifying, or enforcing child support obligations; or enforcing child custody or visitation orders.[3] It required that a designated state agency, directly or by contract, conduct automated comparisons of the Social Security numbers reported by employers to the state directory of new hires and the Social Security numbers of CSE cases that appear in the records of the state registry of child support orders. (The 1996 law required the HHS Secretary to conduct similar comparisons of the federal directories.) When a match occurs the state directory of new hires is required to report to the state CSE agency the name, date of birth, Social Security number of the employee, and employer's name, address, and identification number. The CSE agency then, within 2 business days, instructs appropriate employers to withhold child support obligations from the employee's paycheck, unless the employee's income is not subject to withholding.[4]

Paternity Establishment

Legally identifying the father is a prerequisite for obtaining a child support order. Like previous law, P.L. 104-193 required TANF block grant (Title IV-A) applicants and recipients to cooperate in establishing paternity or obtaining support payments. Moreover, it imposed a penalty for noncooperation; if it is determined that an individual is not cooperating, and the individual does not qualify for any good cause or other exception, then the state must reduce the family's TANF benefit by at least 25% and may remove the family from the TANF program.

P.L. 104-193 also (1) required that paternity be established for 90% of the CSE cases needing such a determination (up from 75%), (2) implemented a simple civil process for establishing paternity, (3) required a uniform affidavit to be completed bymen voluntarily acknowledging paternity and entitles such affidavit to full faith and credit in any state, (4) stipulated that a signed acknowledgment of paternity be considered a legal finding of paternity unless rescinded within 60 days; and thereafter may be challenged in court only on the basis of fraud, duress, or material mistake of fact, (5) provided that no judicial or administrative action is needed to ratify an acknowledgment that is not challenged, and (6) required all parties to submit to genetic testing in contested paternity cases. (See CRS Report RL31467, *Paternity Establishment: Child Support and Beyond.*)

Enforcement

Collection methods used by CSE agencies include income withholding, intercept of federal and state income tax refunds, intercept of unemployment compensation, liens against property, security bonds, and reporting child support obligations to credit bureaus. All jurisdictions also have civil or criminal contempt-of-court procedures and criminal nonsupport laws. Building on legislation (P.L. 102-521) enacted in 1992, P.L. 105-187, the Deadbeat Parents Punishment Act of 1998, established two new federal criminal offenses (subject to a 2-year maximum prison term) with respect to noncustodial parents who repeatedlyfail to financiallysupport children who reside with custodial parents in another state or who flee across state lines to avoid supporting them.

P.L. 104-193 required states to implement expedited procedures that allow them to secure assets to satisfy an arrearage by intercepting or seizing periodic or lump sum payments (such as unemployment and workers' compensation), lotterywinnings, awards, judgements, or settlements, and assets of the debtor parent held by public or private retirement funds, and financial institutions. It required states to implement procedures under which the state would have authorityto withhold, suspend, or restrict use of driver's licenses, professional and occupational licenses, and recreational and sporting licenses of persons who owe past-due support or who fail to comply with subpoenas or warrants relating to paternity or child support proceedings. It also required states to conduct quarterly data matches with financial institutions in the state in order to identify and seize the financial resources of debtor noncustodial parents. P.L. 104-193 authorized the Secretary of State to deny, revoke, or restrict passports of debtor parents. P.L. 104-193 also required states to enact and implement the Uniform Interstate Family Support Act (UIFSA), and expand full faith and credit procedures. P.L. 104-193 also clarified which court has jurisdiction in cases involving multiple child support orders.

Financing

The federal government currently reimburses each state 66% of the cost of administering its CSE program. It also refunds states 90% of the laboratory costs of establishing paternity. In addition, the federal government pays states an incentive payment to encourage them to operate effective programs. P.L. 104-193 required the HHS Secretary in consultation with the state CSE directors to develop a new cost-neutral system of incentive payments to states. P.L. 105-200, the Child Support Performance and Incentive Act of 1998, establishes a new cost-neutral incentive payment system.[5] P.L. 105-200 also replaced the 100% disapproval penalty with reduced financial penalties for states that failed to meet the October 1, 1997 deadline for implementing a CSE statewide automated data processing system.[6]

Collection and Disbursement

Pursuant to P.L. 104-193, as of October 1, 1999, all states were required to have a centralized automated state collection and disbursement unit to which child support payments are paid and from which they are distributed.[7] P.L. 104-193 generally requires employers to remit to the state disbursement unit income withheld within 7 business days after the employee's payday. Further, the state collection and disbursement unit is required to send child support payments to custodial parents with 2 business days of receipt of such payments. (See CRS Report RS20352, *Centralized Collection and Disbursement of Child Support Payments.*)

Distribution of Support

P.L. 104-193 eliminated the $50 passthrough payment (i.e., under old law, the first $50 of current monthly child support payments collected on behalf of an AFDC family was given to the family and disregarded as income to the family so it did not affect the family's AFDC eligibility or benefit status). Once a family went off AFDC, child support arrearage payments generally were divided between the state and federal governments to reimburse them for AFDC; if any money remained, it was given to the family. In contrast, under P.L. 104-193, arrearages that are collected through the federal income tax offset are to be paid to the state (and federal government) and any arrearage payments made by any other method are to be paid to the family first. P.L. 104-193 also included a "hold harmless" provision that required the federal government to assure that a state retains an amount equal to its FY1995 share of support collections. P.L. 106-169 modified the CSE hold harmless provision and repealed it effective October 1, 2001.

Other Provisions

P.L. 104-193 also made changes related to medical support, modification of support orders, collection from federal employees and members of the Armed Forces, fraudulent transfer of property, access and visitation, CSE for Indian tribes, a work requirement for debtor parents, international enforcement, and the placement of Social Security numbers on various license applications.

ISSUES

Restructuring the Financing of the CSE Program

Some policymakers are concerned that the federal government is financing too large a share of CSE costs, and contend that the states should pay a greater share of the program's costs. One consequence of the CSE's financing structure is that the federal government has lost money on the program every year since 1979 and the states (collectively) have made a "profit" on the program every year until FY2000. Before 1989, state "profits" more than compensated for federal losses resulting in a net savings for taxpayers. FY2000 is the first year in which states have not collectively made a "profit" on the CSE program. Some observers argue that any reduction in the federal government's financial commitment to the CSE program could negatively impact states' ability to serve families. Moreover, not all benefits of the program can be measured in money terms. Thus, many argue that indirect savings (i.e., welfare cost avoidance) that occur when a family is kept off "welfare" because of child support collections and the intangible benefits (e.g., personal responsibility and parental involvement of noncustodial parents) make the CSE program socially worthwhile.

Cultivating Parental Involvement to Increase Child Support Collections

Historically, Congress has agreed that visitation and child support should be legally separate issues; and that only child support should be under the purview of the CSE program. Both federal and state policymakers have maintained that denial of visitation rights should be treated separately and should not be considered a reason for stopping child support payments. In recognition of the negative long-term consequences for children associated with the absence of their father, federal, state, and local initiatives to promote financial and personal responsibility of noncustodial parents to their children (e.g., fatherhood initiatives) are receiving more attention. In 1996, P.L. 104-193 provided $10 million per year for grants to states for access and visitation programs, including mediation, counseling, education, and supervised visitation. H.R. 4678, passed by the House on September 7, 2000, included a fatherhood grant program designed to promote marriage, promote successful parenting and the involvement of fathers in the lives of their children, and help fathers improve their economic status by providing them with job-related services. Although the House and Senate did not reach agreement on H.R. 4678, Congress appropriated $3.5 million for a national fatherhood organization called the National Fatherhood Initiative and another $500,000 for a fatherhood organization called the Institute for Responsible Fatherhood and FamilyRevitalization (P.L. 106-553 and P.L. 106-554). Several bills that include fatherhood initiatives have been introduced in the 108th Congress. President Bush's FY2004 budget and H.R. 4, as passed by the House on February 13, 2003, would provide $20 million per year for FY2004-FY2008 in competitive grants to community and faith-based organizations to help noncustodial fathers support their families and become more involved in their children's lives, and to encourage and support healthy marriages and married fatherhood.

Simplifying Distribution Procedures

P.L. 104-193 requires states to pay a higher fraction of child support collections on arrearages to families that have left welfare by making these payments to families first. This has resulted in making an already complicated set of rules for determining who actually gets the child support arrearage payments more complex. (See CRS Report RS20837, *Distribution of Child Support Collections.*) Although some of the complexity ended when the 1996 distribution rules were completely implemented on October 1, 2000, many policymakers contend that Congress should simplify the distribution system which currently requires the tracking of six categories of arrearage payments to properly pay custodial parents. Legislation has been re-introduced in the 108th Congress that would simplify CSE program distribution rules as well as extend the "families first" policy by allowing more child support to go to both ex-welfare families and parents still on welfare. President Bush's FY2004 budget and H.R. 4, as passed by the House on February 13, 2003 would give states incentives (1) to pass through and disregard child support collected on behalf of families receiving TANF benefits and (2) to simplify child support distribution rules so as to benefit families who no longer receive TANF benefits.

REFERENCES

[1]   In FY2002, $118.5 billion in child support obligations ($26.2 billion in current support and $92.3 billion in past-due support) were owed to families receiving CSE services, but only $21.4 billion was paid ($15.1 billion current, $6.3 billion past-due).

[2]   Within 3 business days after receipt of new hire information from the employer, the state directory of new hires is required to furnish the information to the national directory of new hires.

[3]   P.L. 104-193 permitted both custodial and certain noncustodial parents to obtain information from the FPLS. However, P.L. 105-33, the Balanced Budget Act of 1997(which made numerous changes to P.L. 104-193), prohibits FPLS information from being disclosed to noncustodial parents in cases where there is evidence of domestic violence or child abuse and the local court determines that disclosure may result in harm to the custodial parent or child.

[4]   There are three exceptions to the immediate income withholding rule: (1) if one of the parties demonstrates, and the court (or administrative process) finds that there is good cause not to require immediate withholding, (2) if both parties agree in writing to an alternative arrangement, or (3) at the HHS Secretary's discretion, if a state can demonstrate that the rule will not increase the effectiveness or efficiency of the state's CSE program.

[5]   Before FY2002 child support incentive payments were paid out of the federal share of child support collections made on behalf of TANF families. As of October 1, 2001, child support incentive payments are paid with appropriated funds.

[6] Federal CSE law requires suspension of all federal CSE payments to the state when its CSE plan, after appeal, is disapproved. Moreover, states without approved CSE plans could lose funding for the TANF block grant. P.L. 105-200 imposes substantially smaller financial penalties on states that failed to meet the automated data systems requirements. The HHS Secretary is required to reduce the amount the state would otherwise have received in federal child support funding by the penalty amount for the fiscal year in question. The penalty amount percentage is 4% in the case of the first year of noncompliance (FY1998); 8% in the second year (FY1999); 16% in the third year (FY2000); 25% in the fourth year (FY2001); or 30% in the fifth or any subsequent year.

[7] P.L. 106-113 includes a provision that imposes substantially smaller financial penalties on states that failed to meet the centralized collection and disbursement unit requirement. These penalties are identical to those pertaining to failure to meet automated data systems requirements.

In: Family Structure and Support Issues   ISBN: 1-60021-340-5
Editor: A. E. Bennett, pp. 85-93   © 2007 Nova Science Publishers, Inc.

Chapter 6

CHILD SUPPORT PROVISIONS IN THE DEFICIT REDUCTION ACT OF 2005 (P.L. 109-171)*

Carmen Solomon-Fears

ABSTRACT

Among other things, P.L. 109-171 (the budget reconciliation measure, now referred to as the Deficit Reduction Act of 2005 — S. 1932) made a number of changes to the Child Support Enforcement (CSE) program. The act will reduce the federal matching rate for laboratory costs associated with paternity establishment from 90% to 66%, end the federal matching of state expenditures of federal CSE incentive payments reinvested back into the program, and require states to assess a $25 annual user fee for child support services provided to families with no connection to the welfare system. P.L. 109-171 also simplifies CSE distribution rules and extends the "families first" policy by providing incentives to states to encourage them to allow more child support to go to both former welfare families and families still on welfare. In addition, P.L. 109-171 revises some child support enforcement collection mechanisms and adds others. The Congressional Budget Office (CBO) estimates that the CSE provisions contained in P.L. 109-171 will reduce federal costs of the CSE program by $1.5 billion over the five-year period FY2006-FY2010.

---

* Excerpted from CRS Report RS22377, dated February 14, 2006.

BACKGROUND

Over the years, CSE has evolved into a multifaceted program. While recovery of costs to provide cash welfare to needy families with children still remains an important function, other aspects of the program include service delivery and promotion of self-sufficiency and parental responsibility.

The CSE program has helped strengthen families by securing financial support for children from their noncustodial parent on a consistent and continuing basis, and by helping some families to remain self-sufficient and off public assistance by providing the requisite CSE services. Child support payments now are generally recognized as a very important income source for single-parent families. On average, child support constitutes 17% of family income for households that receive it (2001 data). Among poor families who receive it, child support constitutes about 30% of family income (2001 data).

The CSE program, Part D of Title IV of the Social Security Act, was enacted in January 1975 (P.L. 93-647). The CSE program is administered by the Office of Child Support Enforcement (OCSE) in the Department of Health and Human Services (HHS), and funded by general revenues. All 50 states, the District of Columbia, Guam, Puerto Rico, and the Virgin Islands operate CSE programs and are entitled to federal matching funds. The following families automatically qualify for CSE services free of charge: families receiving cash TANF benefits (Title IV-A), foster care payments (Title IV-E), or Medicaid coverage (Title XIX). Collections on behalf of families receiving TANF cash benefits are used to reimburse state and federal governments for TANF payments made to the family. Other families must apply for CSE services, and states must charge an application fee that cannot exceed $25. Child support collected on behalf of nonwelfare families goes to the family, usually through the state disbursement unit.

In 1996, Congress passed major changes to the CSE program as part of its reform of welfare. Since FY2002, when the authorization expired for the Temporary Assistance for Needy Families (TANF) block grant and other related programs, proposals for significant changes to the CSE program have been linked to welfare reauthorization legislation. P.L. 109-171 (the Deficit Reduction Act of 2005, S. 1932),[1] among other things, reauthorized the Temporary Assistance for Needy Families (TANF) block grant and made substantive changes to the CSE program. CBO estimates that the CSE provisions in P.L. 109-171 will reduce federal costs of the CSE program by $1.5 billion over the five-year period FY2006-FY2010. For a comparison of selected provisions, see Table 1.

CHILD SUPPORT ASSIGNMENT AND DISTRIBUTION POLICIES

P.L. 109-171, the Deficit Reduction Act (S. 1932), seeks to improve the CSE program and raise collections in order to increase the economic independence of former welfare families and provide a stable source of income for all single-parent families with a noncustodial parent. It simplifies CSE assignment and distribution rules, and strengthens the "family-first" policies started in the 1996 welfare reform law.

Assignment of Child Support Rights

As a condition of receiving TANF cash benefits, a family must assign its child support rights to the state. Assignment rules determine who has legal claim on the child support payments owed by the noncustodial parent. The child support assignment covers any child support that accrues while the family receives cash TANF benefits, as well as any child support that accrued before the family started receiving TANF benefits. Assigned child support collections are not paid to families; rather, this revenue is kept by states and the federal government as partial reimbursement for welfare benefits. Nonwelfare families who apply for CSE services do not assign their child support rights to the state, and thereby receive all of the child support collected on their behalf. An extremely important feature of the assignment process is the date on which an assignment was entered. If the assignment was entered on or before September 30, 1997, then pre-assistance and during-assistance arrearages are "permanently assigned" to the state. (Note that past-due child support payments are referred to as arrearages.) If the assignment was entered on or after October 1, 1997, then only the arrearages that accumulate while the family receives assistance are "permanently assigned." The family's pre-assistance arrearages are "temporarily assigned," and the right to those arrearages goes back to the family when it leaves TANF, unless the arrearages are collected through the federal income tax refund offset program.

P.L. 109-171 stipulates that the child support assignment only covers child support that accrues while the family receives TANF benefits. This means that any child support arrearages that accrued before the family started receiving TANF benefits would not have to be assigned to the state (even temporarily), and thereby any child support collected on behalf of the former-TANF family for pre-assistance arrearages will go to the family.

Distribution of Child Support

Distribution rules determine which claim is paid first when a child support collection occurs. The order of payment of the child support collection is important because in many cases arrearages are never fully paid.

TANF Families

While a family receives TANF cash benefits, the states and federal government retain any current support and any assigned arrearages collected up to the cumulative amount of TANF benefits that has been paid to the family. While states may pay their share of collections to the family, they must pay the federal government the federal government's share of child support collections collected on behalf of TANF families. This means that the state, and not the federal government, bears the entire cost of any child support passed through to families and disregarded by the state in determining the family's TANF cash benefit.

P.L. 109-171 provides incentives in the form of federal cost sharing to states to direct more of the child support collected on behalf of TANF families to the families themselves (often referred to as a "family-first" policy), as opposed to using such collections to reimburse state and federal coffers for welfare benefits paid to the families. P.L. 109-171 will help states pay for the cost of their CSE pass-through and disregard policies by requiring the federal government to share in the costs of the entire amount of child support collections passed through and disregarded by states. P.L. 109-171 will allow states to pay up to $100 per month (or $200 per month to a family with two or more children) in child support collected on behalf of a TANF or foster care family to the family, and would not require the state to pay the federal government the federal share of those payments. In order for the federal government to share in the cost of the child support pass-through, the state would be required to disregard (i.e., not count) the child support collection paid to the family in determining the family's cash TANF benefit. CBO estimates that this provision will cost the federal government $140 million over the five-year period FY2006-2010. This provision takes effect on October 1, 2008.

Former TANF Families

Pursuant to the 1996 welfare reform law (P.L. 104-193), beginning on October 1, 2000, states must distribute to former TANF families the following child support collections first before the state and the federal government are reimbursed (the "family-first" policy): (1) all current child support, (2) any child support arrearages that accrue after the family leaves TANF (these arrearages are called never-assigned arrearages), plus (3) any arrearages that accrued before the family began receiving TANF benefits. Any child support arrearages that accrue during the time the family is on TANF belong to the state and federal government.

One of the goals of the 1996 welfare reform law with regard to CSE distribution provisions was to create a distribution priority that favored families once they leave the TANF rolls. Thus, generally speaking, under current law, child support that accrues before a family receives TANF and after the family stops receiving TANF goes to the family, whereas child support that accrues while the family is receiving TANF goes to the state. This additional family income is expected to reduce dependence on public assistance by both promoting exit from TANF and preventing entry and re-entry to TANF.

P.L. 109-171 gives states the option of distributing to former TANF families the full amount of child support collected on their behalf (i.e., both current support and all child support arrearages — including arrearages collected through the federal income tax refund offset program). Thereby, P.L. 109-171 allows states to simplify the CSE distribution process by eliminating the special treatment of child support arrearages collected through the federal income tax refund offset program. Under P.L. 109-171, the federal government shares with the states the costs of paying child support arrearages to the family first. CBO estimates that this provision will cost the federal government $283 million over the five-year period FY2006-2010. This provision takes effect on October 1, 2009, or at state option not before October 1, 2008.

EXPANSION OR ENHANCEMENT OF COLLECTION/ENFORCEMENT TOOLS

The CSE program has numerous methods by which to obtain child support from noncustodial parents. They include income withholding; interception of federal and state income tax refunds; seizure of lump-sum benefits, lottery winnings, and settlements; withholding of driver's licenses, professional licenses, and recreational licenses of persons who owe past-due child support; seizure of assets from banks and other financial institutions; denial of passports; imposition of criminal penalties against noncustodial parents who repeatedly fail to financially support children who reside with custodial parents in another state; and civil or criminal contempt-of-court procedures. Nonetheless, in FY2004, states were collecting only 18% of child support obligations for which they collectively had responsibility. For several years, child advocates and Members of Congress have been pushing for more or enhanced CSE tools.

P.L. 109-171 includes provisions that (1) lower the threshold amount for denial of a passport to a noncustodial parent who owes past-due child support; (2) allow states to use the federal income tax refund offset program to collect past-due child support for persons not on TANF who are no longer minors; (3) authorize the Secretary of HHS to compare information of noncustodial parents who owe past-due child support with information maintained by insurers concerning insurance payments and to furnish any information resulting from a match to CSE agencies so that they can pursue child support arrearages; (4) allow an assisting state to establish a CSE interstate case based on another state's request for assistance (thereby enabling an assisting state to use the CSE statewide automated data processing and information retrieval system for interstate cases); (5) require states to review and, if appropriate, adjust child support orders of TANF families every three years; and (6) require that medical child support for a child be provided by either or both parents. CBO estimates that these CSE collection tools will reduce federal costs by about $36 million over the period FY2006-2010. (The effective dates related to collection techniques vary; a few take effect immediately, while others take effect between October 1, 2006, and October 1, 2009.)

FINANCING PROVISIONS

The federal government reimburses each state 66% of the cost of its CSE program. However, it reimburses states at a higher 90% matching rate for the laboratory costs of establishing paternity. In addition, the federal government pays states an incentive payment[2] to encourage them to operate effective programs.

P.L. 109-171 includes provisions that (1) establish a $25 annual user fee for individuals who have never been on TANF but receive CSE services and who have received at least $500 in any given year — saving the federal government $172 million over the five-year period FY2006-2010; (2) reduce the CSE federal matching rate for the laboratory costs associated with establishing paternity from 90% to 66%[3] — saving $28 million over the five years; and (3) eliminate the federal match on CSE incentive payments that states, in compliance with federal law, reinvest back into the CSE program — saving $1.6 billion over the five years.[4]

Table 1. Comparison of Child Support Assignment, Distribution, and Financing Rules Under Old and New Law

	Old Law	New Law (P.L. 109-171)
Child Support Assignment Rules	Assignment rules stipulate who has a legal claim on the child support payments owed by the noncustodial parent. Generally, child support owed before and during a family's time on TANF belongs to the state and federal government, and child support owed after the family leaves the TANF rolls belongs to the family.	Stipulates that the child support assignment only covers child support that accrues during the period that the family receives TANF. Thus, child support owed before a family enrolls in TANF and after the family leaves TANF belongs to the family, and child support owed during the time the family is on TANF belongs to the state. Effective October 1, 2009; October 1, 2008, at state option.
Child Support Distribution Rules	Child support distribution rules determine the order in which child support collections are paid when both the family and the state have competing claims on the money. The general rule is that if the family is on TANF (or receives federal foster care aid), then the state is paid first. While a family receives cash TANF benefits, the state can send some, all, or none of its share of the child support collected to the family. The state is required to send the federal government the federal share of any child support collected on behalf of TANF families.

If the family is not on TANF, then the family is paid first. However, an exception occurs for former TANF families if the child support is collected via the federal income tax refund offset program, in such cases, the state is paid first. | For families who receive assistance from the state (TANF or foster care), requires the federal government to waive its share of the child support collections passed through to TANF families by the state and disregarded by the state — up to an amount equal to $100 per month in the case of a family with one child, and up to $200 per month in the case of a family with two or more children. Effective October 1, 2008.

Simplifies child support distribution rules to give states the option of providing families that have left TANF the full amount of the child support collected on their behalf (i.e., both current child support and child support arrearages, including support payments collected via the federal income tax refund offset program). The federal government would have to share with the states the costsof paying child support arrearages to the family first. Effective October 1, 2009; October 1, 2008 at state option. |

Table 1. Continued

	Old Law	New Law (P.L. 109-171)
Financing Rules	Welfare families are automatically enrolled free of charge in the CSE program. Nonwelfare families must apply for CSE services, and states must charge an application fee that cannot exceed $25.	Requires families that have never been on TANF to pay a $25 annual user fee when child support enforcement efforts on their behalf are successful (i.e., at least $500 annually is collected on their behalf). Effective October 1, 2006.
	In general, the federal government reimburses each state 66% of the cost of expenditures on its CSE program. However, for the laboratory costs of establishing paternity, the federal government reimburses states at a higher 90% matching rate.	Reduces the federal matching rate for laboratory costs incurred in determining paternity from 90% to 66%. Effective October 1, 2006.
	In addition, the federal government pays states an incentive payment to encourage them to operate effective programs. Federal law requires states to reinvest CSE incentive payments back into the CSE program or related activities. If incentive payments are reinvested in the CSE program, they are reimbursed at the appropriate CSE federal matching rate, i.e., 66% for general activities or 90% for laboratory testing for paternity determination.	Prohibits federal matching of state expenditure of federal CSE incentive payments. (This means that CSE incentive payments that are received by states and reinvested in the CSE program are not eligible for federal reimbursement.) Effective October 1, 2007.

REFERENCES

[1]   The conference agreement on S. 1932, the Deficit Reduction Act of 2005 (H.Rept. 109-362), was originally passed by the House on December 19, 2005. It was then passed by the Senate with amendments on December 21,

2005, and subsequently was passed again by the House on February 1, 2006. It was signed into law (P.L. 109-171) by the President on February 8, 2006.

[2]   The CSE incentive payment was statutorily set by P.L. 105-200. In the aggregate, incentive payments to states may not exceed $446 million for FY2005, $458 million for FY2006, $471 million for FY2007, and $483 million for FY2008, to be increased to account for inflation in years thereafter. The incentive payment is based in part on five performance measures related to establishment of paternity and child support orders, collection of current and past-due child support payments, and cost-effectiveness. In addition, P.L. 105-200 required mandatory reinvestment of child support incentive payments into the CSE program or related activities.

[3]   Paternity establishment costs that are not associated with laboratory testing are reimbursed at the regular CSE federal matching rate of 66%.

[4]   In addition, P.L. 109-171 establishes a minimum funding level for technical assistance and the Federal Parent Locator Service (FPLS) — costing $4 million over the five-year period FY2006-FY2010. P.L. 109-171 prevents funding for technical assistance (which is equal to 1% of the federal share of child support collected on behalf of TANF families) from going below the amount the state received in FY2002. Similarly, P.L. 109-171 prevents funding for the FPLS (which is equal to 2% of the federal share of child support collected on behalf of TANF families) from going below the amount the state received in FY2002. It is expected that the diminishing share of the CSE caseload that receives cash TANF benefits, together with the new rules related to assignment and distribution, will result in the federal government receiving a smaller amount of child support collections than it previously received.

In: Family Structure and Support Issues
Editor: A. E. Bennett, pp. 95-102

Chapter 7

THE FAMILY AND MEDICAL LEAVE ACT: BACKGROUND AND U.S. SUPREME COURT CASES*

Jon O. Shimabukuro

ABSTRACT

This chapter provides background on the eligibility and notification requirements for taking leave under the Family and Medical Leave Act ("FMLA"). The FMLA guarantees eligible employees 12 workweeks of unpaid leave for the birth or adoption of a child; for the placement of a foster child; for the care of a spouse, child, or parent suffering from a serious health condition; or for a serious health condition that makes the employee unable to perform the functions of the employee's position. Since the FMLA's enactment in 1993, the U.S. Supreme Court has considered two cases involving the statute. *Ragsdale v. Wolverine World Wide, Inc.* and *Nevada Department of Human Resources v. Hibbs* are discussed in this chapter. The report will be updated in response to the FMLA's amendment and relevant Supreme Court cases.

The Family and Medical Leave Act ("FMLA") guarantees eligible employees 12 workweeks of unpaid leave for certain specified reasons.[1] Enacted in 1993, the FMLA seeks "to balance the demands of the workplace with the needs of families, to promote the stability and economic security of families, and to promote national interests in preserving family integrity."[2]

---

* Excerpted from CRS Report RS22090, dated March 23, 2005.

This chapter provides background on the eligibility and notification requirements for taking leave under the FMLA, and discusses U.S. Supreme Court cases that have considered the validity of FMLA regulations and the availability of money damages under the FMLA for state employees.

BACKGROUND

Section 102(a)(1) of the FMLA provides that an eligible employee shall be entitled to a total of 12 workweeks of leave during any 12-month period for one or more of the following reasons:

1. Because of the birth of a son or daughter of the employee and in order to care for such son or daughter;
2. Because of the placement of a son or daughter with the employee for adoption or foster care;
3. In order to care for the spouse, or a son, daughter, or parent, of the employee, if such spouse, son, daughter, or parent has a serious health condition;
4. Because of a serious health condition that makes the employee unable to perform the functions of the position of such employee.[3]

The FMLA defines an "eligible employee" as one who has been employed for at least 12 months by the employer from whom leave is requested, and who has been employed for at least 1,250 hours of service with such employer during the previous 12-month period.[4] The FMLA applies only to employers engaged in commerce or in an industry affecting commerce who have at least 50 employees who are employed for each working day during each of 20 or more calendar workweeks in the current or preceding calendar year.[5]

Most employees who take leave under the FMLA shall be entitled, upon their return, to be restored to their positions of employment or to equivalent positions with equivalent employment benefits, pay, and other terms and conditions of employment.[6] During the leave period, an employer shall maintain the employee's coverage in any group health plan at the level and under the same conditions that would have existed had the employee continued in employment.[7]

Certain highly compensated employees may be denied restoration to their prior positions under specified circumstances. A salaried employee who is among the highest paid 10 percent of employees employed within 75 miles of the facility at which he is employed may be denied restoration to his prior position when the denial is necessary to prevent "substantial and grievous economic injury" to the employer's operations, the employer notifies the employee of its intent not to restore the employee to his prior position, and, in a case in which leave has commenced, the employee elects not to return after receiving such notice.[8]

When the necessity for leave is foreseeable because of a serious health condition and a planned medical treatment, the FMLA requires the employee to make a reasonable effort to schedule the treatment so as not to unduly disrupt the operations of the employer.[9] In addition, the employee is required to notify the employer of his intention to take leave not less than 30 days before the date the leave is to begin.[10] If the date of the treatment requires leave to begin in less than 30 days, the employee shall provide such notice as is practicable.[11] If an employee fails to provide 30 days notice for foreseeable leave, with no reasonable excuse for the delay, the employer may delay the taking of leave until at least 30 days after the date the employee provides notice to the employer.[12] An employer may also delay leave if an employee fails to provide medical certification to substantiate the need for leave because of a serious health condition.[13]

While the FMLA guarantees leave for eligible employees, it also permits an employer to substitute an employee's accrued paid vacation leave, personal leave, or family leave for the leave provided under the statute for the birth or adoption of a child, or for the care of a child, spouse, or parent who has a serious health condition.[14] In addition, an employer may substitute an employee's accrued paid vacation leave, personal leave, or medical or sick leave for the leave provided under the FMLA for the employee's own serious health condition.[15] An employer who substitutes vacation leave, personal leave, family leave, or medical or sick leave for the leave provided under the statute must tell the employee that the paid leave is being designated as FMLA leave.[16]

Section 107(a)(2) of the FMLA provides a private right of action for employees who are denied their rights under the statute.[17] The private right of action may be limited by the filing of a complaint by the Secretary of Labor on behalf of the employee.[18]

THE FMLA AND THE U.S. SUPREME COURT

The Supreme Court has considered two cases involving the FMLA since the statute's enactment. In *Ragsdale v. Wolverine World Wide, Inc.*, the Court considered the validity of a FMLA regulation which provided that if an employee takes paid or unpaid leave and the employer does not designate the leave as FMLA leave, the leave taken would not count against the employee's FMLA entitlement.[19] Wolverine World Wide maintained a leave plan that permitted its employees up to seven months of unpaid sick leave. Ragsdale was terminated after her request for additional leave beyond the seven-month allowance was exhausted, and she was unable to return to work. Because Wolverine World Wide never informed Ragsdale that 12 weeks of leave under the leave plan would count as her FMLA leave, Ragsdale sought relief based on the FMLA regulation.

While the Court recognized that the Secretary of Labor's judgment in issuing the regulation must be given considerable weight, it also acknowledged that the regulation could not stand if it was "'arbitrary, capricious, or manifestly contrary to the statute.'"[20] In this case, the Court maintained that the regulation was invalid because it altered the FMLA's cause of action in a fundamental way: "[The regulation] transformed the company's failure to give notice – along with its refusal to grant her more . . . leave – into an actionable violation . . ."[21]

The Court noted that to prevail under FMLA's enforcement provisions, an employee must prove, as a threshold matter, that the employer interfered with, restrained, or denied the exercise of FMLA rights. Moreover, the Court observed that even when an employer has engaged in such misconduct, the FMLA does not provide relief unless the employee has been prejudiced by the violation.[22] The FMLA regulation at issue established an "irrebuttable presumption" that an employee's exercise of FMLA rights was impaired without any empirical or logical basis for the presumption.[23] Although Wolverine World Wide had granted Ragsdale more than 12 weeks of leave, the regulation, if upheld, would permit her to obtain reinstatement and the other relief provided under the statute. By granting such relief "absent a showing of consequential harm, the regulation worked an end run around important limitations of the statute's remedial scheme."[24] The Court contended that the regulation "relieves employees of the burden of proving any real impairment of their rights and resulting prejudice."[25]

In *Nevada Department of Human Resources v. Hibbs*, the Court concluded that state employees could recover money damages from a state in federal court for violation of section 102(a)(1)(C) of the FMLA.[26] Hibbs was terminated after he failed to return to work with the Nevada Department of Human Resources' Welfare Division after being told that he had exhausted his FMLA leave. The Court considered the case to resolve a split among the U.S. Courts of Appeals on the question of whether an individual may sue a state for money damages in federal court for violation of section 102(a)(1)(C).

Although the Constitution does not provide generally for federal jurisdiction over suits against nonconsenting states, it is understood that Congress may abrogate a state's immunity in federal court if it makes its intention "unmistakably clear in the language of the statute and acts pursuant to a valid exercise of its power under section 5 of the Fourteenth Amendment."[27] Because the language of the FMLA provides clearly for an employee to seek relief in any federal or state court of competent jurisdiction against a public agency, the Court focused on whether Congress acted within its constitutional authority when it sought to abrogate the states' immunity.[28]

Section 5 of the Fourteenth Amendment grants Congress the power to enforce the substantive guarantees of section 1 of the Fourteenth Amendment, including equal protection of the laws, by enacting "appropriate legislation."[29] In the exercise of its authority under section 5, Congress may enact "prophylactic" legislation that proscribes facially constitutional conduct as a way of preventing and deterring unconstitutional conduct.[30] However, to be valid, such legislation must exhibit "'congruence and proportionality between the injury to be prevented or remedied and the means adopted to that end.'"[31]

The FMLA operates to protect the right to be free from gender-based discrimination in the workplace.[32] A review of the FMLA's legislative record by the Court indicated that stereotype-based beliefs about the allocation of family duties still existed at the time of the measure's enactment. Employers continued to rely on those beliefs to establish discriminatory leave policies.[33] Moreover, Congress recognized that the state leave policies that existed prior to the FMLA's enactment were limited and would do little to combat stereotypes about the roles of male and female employees.[34] For example, prior to the FMLA's enactment, seven states had childcare leave provisions that applied only to women.[35] Given these findings, the Court concluded that Congress was justified in enacting the FMLA as remedial legislation: "In sum, the States' record of unconstitutional participation in, and fostering of, gender-based discrimination in the administration of leave benefits is weighty enough to justify the enactment of prophylactic [section] 5 legislation."[36]

Focusing specifically on section 102(a)(1)(C), the Court maintained that the provision is congruent and proportional to the targeted violation: "the FMLA is narrowly targeted at the fault line between work and family – precisely where sex-based overgeneralization has been and remains strongest – and affects only one aspect of the employment relationship."[37] The Court also cited the FMLA's limitations as evidence of its being congruent and proportional. For example, the statute applies only to employees who meet specified tenure requirements. Employees must give advance notice of foreseeable leave. 12 weeks, rather than a longer period, was selected as the appropriate leave floor. These and other limitations led the Court to find that section 102(a)(1) is "congruent and proportional to its remedial object, and can 'be understood as responsive to, or designed to prevent, unconstitutional behavior.'"[38]

Because the FMLA was found to be a valid exercise of Congress's power under section 5 of the Fourteenth Amendment, and because the statute provides clearly for relief against a public agency, including the government of a state or political subdivision, the Court concluded that money damages are available to state employees when the state fails to comply with the FMLA.

REFERENCES

[1]   29 U.S.C. §§ 2601-2654.

[2]   29 U.S.C. § 2601(b)(1), (b)(2).

[3]   29 U.S.C. § 2612(a)(1).

[4]   29 U.S.C. § 2611(2). The term "eligible employee" does not include most federal employees. Federal employees are covered generally under the Federal Employees Family Friendly Leave Act ("FEFFLA"). See also 5 U.S.C. § 6307(d) (permitting the use of sick leave to care for a family member having an illness or injury, and to make arrangements for or to attend the funeral of a family member).

[5]   29 U.S.C. § 2611(4)(I). See also 29 U.S.C. §2611(2)(B)(ii) (Employers who employ 50 or more employees within a 75-mile radius of an employee's worksite are subject to the FMLA even if they may have fewer than 50 employees at a single worksite.).

[6]   29 U.S.C. § 2614(a)(1).

[7]   29 U.S.C. § 2614(c)(1).

[8]   29 U.S.C. § 2614(b)(1), (b)(2).

[9]   29 U.S.C. § 2612(e)(2)(A).

[10]   29 U.S.C. § 2612(e)(2)(B).

[11]   *Id.*

[12]   29 C.F.R. § 825.304(b).

[13]   29 C.F.R. § 825.312(b).

[14]   29 U.S.C. § 2612(d)(A).

[15]   29 U.S.C. § 2612(d)(B).

[16]   29 C.F.R. § 825.208.

[17]   29 U.S.C. § 2617(a)(2). See also 29 U.S.C. § 2615.

[18]   29 U.S.C. § 2617(a)(4).

[19]   535 U.S. 81 (2002). 29 C.F.R. § 825.700(a) (1991) provided, in relevant part: "If an employee takes paid or unpaid leave and the employer does not

designate the leave as FMLA leave, the leave taken does not count against an employee's FMLA entitlement."

[20] *Id.* at 86 (quoting *Chevron U.S.A. Inc. v. Natural Resources Defense Council, Inc.*, 467 U.S. 837, 844 (1984)).

[21] *Ragsdale*, 535 U.S. at 91.

[22] *Ragsdale*, 535 U.S. at 89.

[23] *Ragsdale*, 535 U.S. at 90.

[24] *Ragsdale*, 535 U.S. at 91.

[25] *Ragsdale*, 535 U.S. at 90.

[26] 538 U.S. 721 (2003). Section 102(a)(1)(C) of the FMLA entitles an eligible employee to take 12 workweeks of leave during any 12-month period to care for such employee's child, spouse, or parent with a serious health condition. For additional information about *Nevada Department of Human Resources v. Hibbs*, see CRS Report RL31604, *Suits Against State Employers Under the Family and Medical Leave Act: Analysis of Nevada Department of Human Resources v. Hibbs*.

[27] *Hibbs*, 538 U.S. at 726. See also *Board of Trustees of Univ. of Ala. v. Garrett*, 531 U.S. 356 (2001); *Blatchford v. Native Village of Noatak*, 501 U.S. 775 (1991). In enacting the FMLA, Congress relied on its power under section 5 of the Fourteenth Amendment, as well as its authority under the Commerce Clause of Article I. However, Congress may not abrogate the states' sovereign immunity pursuant to its Article I power over commerce.

[28] See 29 U.S.C. § 2611(4)(A)(iii) ("The term 'employer' – includes any 'public agency', as defined in section 203(x) of this title."). 29 U.S.C. § 203(x) defines the term "public employer" to mean "the Government of the United States; the government of a State or political subdivision thereof; any agency of the United States (including the United States Postal Service and Postal Rate Commission), a State, or a political subdivision of a State; or any interstate governmental agency."

[29] U.S. Const. amend. XIV, § 5.

[30] *Hibbs*, 538 U.S. at 727-28.

[31] *Hibbs*, 538 U.S. at 728 (quoting *City of Boerne v. Flores*, 521 U.S. 507, 520 (1997)).

[32] See 29 U.S.C. § 2601(b)(4) (explaining that one of the purposes of the FMLA is to minimize the potential for employment discrimination on the basis of sex by ensuring that leave is available for eligible medical reasons and for compelling family reasons on a gender-neutral basis).

[33] *Hibbs*, 538 U.S. at 730.

[34] *Hibbs*, 538 U.S. at 733-34.

[35] *Hibbs*, 538 U.S. at 733.

[36] *Hibbs*, 538 U.S. at 735.

[37] *Hibbs*, 538 U.S. at 738.

[38] *Hibbs*, 538 U.S. at 739-40 (quoting *City of Boerne v. Flores*, 521 U.S. 507, 532 (1997)).

In: Family Structure and Support Issues
Editor: A. E. Bennett, pp. 103-110

ISBN: 1-60021-340-5
© 2007 Nova Science Publishers, Inc.

Chapter 8

PARENTAL NOTIFICATION AND AYOTTE V. PLANNED PARENTHOOD OF NORTHERN NEW ENGLAND[*]

Jon O. Shimabukuro

ABSTRACT

This chapter discusses *Ayotte v. Planned Parenthood of Northern New England*, which will be decided by the U.S. Supreme Court this term. The case involves the constitutionality of the New Hampshire Parental Notification Prior to Abortion Act. In November 2004, the U.S. Court of Appeals for the First Circuit invalidated the act because it does not include an explicit exception that would waive the measure's requirements to preserve the health of the pregnant minor. Ayotte, the Attorney General of New Hampshire, contends that a judicial bypass procedure included in the act and other state statutes sufficiently preserve the health of a minor. The Court will review that position, and consider whether the First Circuit applied the correct standard of review when it heard the case in 2004.

In *Ayotte v. Planned Parenthood of Northern New England*, the U.S. Supreme Court will consider whether the New Hampshire Parental Notification Prior to Abortion Act (the "Act") may be upheld despite its lack of an explicit exception

---

[*] Excerpted from CRS Report RS22342, dated December 2, 2005.

that would waive the act's requirements to preserve the health of a pregnant minor. In past abortion cases, the Court has discussed requiring such an exception in measures that regulate abortion at the pre-and postviability stages of pregnancy. In November 2004, the U.S. Court of Appeals for the First Circuit concluded that the act is unconstitutional because it does not include a health exception. The case was argued before the U.S. Supreme Court on November 30, 2005, and a decision is expected in 2006.

Under the act, no abortion shall be performed upon an unemancipated minor or female for whom a guardian or conservator has been appointed until at least 48 hours after written notice has been delivered to one parent of the minor.[1] While the act includes several exceptions to the notification requirement, including a judicial bypass procedure and a waiver of the requirement if the attending abortion provider certifies that the abortion is necessary to prevent the minor's death and there is insufficient time to provide the required notice (the so-called "death exception"), it does not include an explicit waiver that would allow an abortion to be performed to protect the health of the minor.

Ayotte, the Attorney General of New Hampshire, contends that the act's judicial bypass procedure and other state statutes sufficiently preserve the health of the minor. However, Planned Parenthood of Northern New England and the other respondents maintain that the act must have a health exception.

Ayotte also argues that the First Circuit failed to apply the correct standard of review when it heard the case in 2004. The respondents brought a "facial challenge" to the act. Unlike an "as applied" challenge, which considers the effect of a measure as applied to a particular individual, a facial challenge attempts to invalidate a measure before it takes effect. Rather than apply a more rigorous standard that was first articulated by the Court in a 1987 case, the First Circuit applied the undue burden standard recognized by the Court in *Planned Parenthood of Southeastern Pennsylvania v. Casey*.[2] The Court's decision in *Ayotte* is expected to clarify which standard should be used in facial challenges to abortion measures.

HEALTH EXCEPTION

The need for a health exception in abortion regulations was first discussed in *Roe v. Wade*. With regard to the State's interest in protecting fetal life after viability, the Court indicated that a State "may go so far as to proscribe abortion during that period, except when it is necessary to preserve the life or health of the mother."[3] In *Stenberg v. Carhart*, a 2000 case involving the so-called "partial-birth" abortion procedure, the Court appeared to extend the health exception requirement to previability abortion regulation: "Since the law requires a health exception in order to validate even a postviability abortion regulation, it at a minimum requires the same in respect to previability regulation."[4]

The respondents first challenged the act shortly after its passage in June 2003. In December 2003, a federal district court in New Hampshire concluded that the act is unconstitutional because it lacks a health exception and because its so-called "death exception" is too narrow. The court noted that "on its face, the act does not comply with the constitutional requirement that laws restricting a woman's access to abortion must provide a health exception."[5] The court found that other New Hampshire statutes do not provide an alternative health exception that could render the act constitutional. In addition, the court maintained that the act's judicial bypass procedure does not "save the act from the lack of a constitutionally required health exception."[6]

On appeal, the Attorney General defended the act and its lack of a health exception on four grounds. First, the Attorney General argued that parental notification statutes do not require a health exception because of the interests that are protected by these statutes; that is, while a health exception is necessary for a statute that prohibits a particular method of abortion, it is not needed in a parental notification statute that protects minors from undertaking the risks of abortion without the advice and support of a parent. The First Circuit disagreed with the Attorney General, maintaining that the interests served by a statute do not have an impact on the need for a health exception: "[R]egardless of the interests served by New Hampshire's parental notice statute, it does not escape the Constitution's requirement of a health exception."[7]

The Attorney General's second argument focused on *Hodgson v. Minnesota*, a 1990 case in which the Court upheld Minnesota's parental notification statute despite the absence of a health exception. The Attorney General contended that the court's decision should be controlled by *Hodgson*. However, the First Circuit noted that the lack of a health exception was not raised as a reason to invalidate the statute at issue in *Hodgson*. Moreover, the First Circuit reasoned that even if the Court had considered the absence of a health exception in *Hodgson*, the Court's subsequent decisions in *Casey* and *Stenberg* would now require a health exception in the New Hampshire statute.

The Attorney General's remaining arguments were similar to those made before the district court. Acknowledging that the act contains no explicit health exception, the Attorney General argued that other provisions of New Hampshire law provide a functional equivalent. The Attorney General identified various statutes that preclude civil and criminal liability for health professionals who provide care under certain circumstances. For example, under one statute, a physician would be shielded from criminal liability if he provides emergency medical care when no one competent to consent to such care is available. Similarly, another statute would preclude civil liability for health professionals who render emergency medical care without consent.

The First Circuit concluded that the proffered statutes would not preclude all civil and criminal liability for medical personnel who violate the act's notice requirements to preserve a minor's health. While the statutes would protect medical personnel who provide treatment without consent, they would not necessarily protect such individuals when treatment is provided to a consenting minor without the parental notice required by the act. Moreover, the First Circuit indicated that the clear and unambiguous language of the act identifies only three exceptions to the parental notice requirement: when abortion is necessary to prevent the minor's death; when a parent certifies in writing that he or she has been notified; and when a court grants a judicial bypass. The First Circuit reasoned that it would be contrary to basic canons of statutory construction to construe other statutory provisions, like those identified by the Attorney General, as superceding the clear intent of the act and allowing other opportunities to avoid the notice requirement.

Finally, the Attorney General argued that the act's judicial bypass procedure preserves a minor's health by allowing for the prompt authorization of a health-related abortion without notice. The act's judicial bypass procedure provides for the prompt consideration of cases involving minors who do not want a parent to be notified. Under the act, a minor is afforded 24-hour, 7-day access to the courts, and a court must rule on a minor's petition within seven calendar days from the time a petition is filed. If a decision is appealed, a ruling must be issued within seven calendar days.

The First Circuit was not convinced that the judicial bypass procedure adequately protects a minor's health: "Delays of up to two weeks can . . . occur, during which time a minor's health may be adversely affected. Even when the courts act as expeditiously as possible, those minors who need an immediate abortion to protect their health are at risk."[8] The First Circuit determined that the bypass procedure could not replace the constitutionally required health exception because of the potential delay.

DEATH EXCEPTION

The First Circuit affirmed the district court's decision with respect to the act's death exception. The First Circuit maintained that the exception is too narrow and fails to safeguard a physician's good-faith medical determination concerning whether a minor's life is at risk. Because the course of medical complications cannot be predicted with precision, a physician cannot always determine whether death will occur within the 48-hour time period contemplated by the act. Consequently, the death exception forces a physician to gamble with a patient's life in hopes of complying with the notice requirement, or risk violating the act by providing an abortion without parental notification. The First Circuit believed that the threat of sanctions that arises from such a choice would have a chilling effect on the willingness of physicians to perform abortions when a minor's life is at risk. The court also found that the absence of a clear standard by which to judge a physician's decision to perform an abortion would have a similar chilling effect on a physician's willingness to provide lifesaving abortions.

STANDARD OF REVIEW

The Attorney General has asked the Court to consider whether the First Circuit applied the correct standard of review to the respondents' "facial challenge" of the act. In *United States v. Salerno*, a 1987 case involving a facial challenge to the Bail Reform Act, the Court determined that facial challenges require the challenger to establish that "no set of circumstances exists" under which a measure would be valid.[9] The *Salerno* standard requires that a measure be upheld even if it operates unconstitutionally under some circumstances.

Application of the *Salerno* standard, however, has been complicated by the Court's adoption of the undue burden standard in *Casey*. In *Casey* and *Stenberg*, the Court applied the undue burden standard to invalidate state restrictions on abortion. Among federal courts of appeals, only the Fifth Circuit has continued to apply the *Salerno* standard to facial challenges to abortion regulations. The undue burden standard is believed by some to be a less stringent standard because it would render an abortion regulation facially invalid if "in a large fraction of cases . . . it will operate as a substantial obstacle to a woman's choice to undergo an abortion."[10]

While the First Circuit acknowledged that the Court has never explicitly addressed the tension between the *Salerno* standard and the undue burden standard, it concluded that the act should be subject to the undue burden standard. The First Circuit was persuaded by the Court's application of that standard in *Casey* and *Stenberg*, as well as the use of the standard by a significant number of the courts of appeals.

The Attorney General maintains that the First Circuit should have applied the *Salerno* standard when it evaluated the act. The Attorney General has cited *Ohio v. Akron Center for Reproductive Health* and *Rust v. Sullivan*, two abortion cases from 1990 and 1991 in which the Court applied the *Salerno* standard, to support its position that the *Salerno* standard is appropriate for evaluating abortion regulations.[11] Moreover, the Attorney General argues that the *Salerno* standard is consistent with the Court's traditional practice of adjudicating constitutional questions only in concrete cases and controversies.

The respondents, however, insist that facial invalidation of the act is the only relief that effectively protects the health of minors. They argue that minors challenging the act on an as applied basis would have to "delay getting appropriate and urgently needed medical treatment until they get a constitutional ruling permitting it."[12]

The Court's application of the undue burden standard in *Casey* and *Stenberg* would seem to suggest that it no longer views the *Salerno* standard as appropriate for evaluating facial challenges to abortion regulations. The Court's refusal to review four abortion decisions in which the undue burden standard and not the *Salerno* standard was applied may further suggest that the Court endorses the use of the undue burden standard.[13]

The absence of a definitive statement by the Court concerning the *Salerno* standard and its application to abortion regulations following *Casey* has prompted considerable interest in *Ayotte*. If the Court reaffirms the use of the *Salerno* standard in abortion cases, the wholesale invalidation of future abortion statutes seems unlikely. Individual plaintiffs would have to challenge the constitutionality of an abortion measure as it was applied to them. Delays that could accompany a plaintiff's case would likely raise concerns about the possibility that a woman's health was being compromised.

In addition, a determination by the Court that an explicit health exception is not necessary because of the act's judicial bypass procedure and other New Hampshire statutes would also be significant. Such a decision would likely have an impact on the parental consent and notification laws that exist in forty-four states.[14] It would seem possible that some state legislatures would amend their consent and notification requirements to remove existing health exceptions.

Questions posed by some of the justices during the oral argument on *Ayotte* seem to suggest that the Court might be willing to remand the case to the First

Circuit to recognize a health exception that would then make the act constitutional. It is uncertain how the court would fashion such an exception. Responding to the justices' questions, counsel for the respondents indicated that allowing the First Circuit to find a health exception for the act would likely have the effect of encouraging states to write patently unconstitutional laws with the knowledge that a reviewing court would later correct any constitutional flaws. A remand of the case is not guaranteed. It is still possible that the Court could invalidate the act because of its lack of an explicit health exception. The Court's decision is not expected until 2006.

REFERENCES

[1]   N.H. Rev. Stat. Ann. § 132:25.

[2]   For additional discussion of *Planned Parenthood of Southeastern Pennsylvania v. Casey* and other abortion decisions, see CRS Issue Brief IB95095, *Abortion: Legislative Response*, by Karen J. Lewis and Jon O. Shimabukuro.

[3]   410 U.S. 113, 163-64 (1973).

[4]   530 U.S. 914, 930 (2000).

[5]   *Planned Parenthood of Northern New England v. Heed*, 296 F.Supp.2d 59, 65 (D. N.H. 2003).

[6]   *Heed*, 296 F.Supp.2d at 66.

[7]   *Planned Parenthood of Northern New England v. Heed*, 390 F.3d 53, 60 (1st Cir. 2004).

[8]   *Heed*, 390 F.3d at 62.

[9]   481 U.S. 739, 745 (1987).

[10]   *Planned Parenthood of Southeastern Pennsylvania v. Casey*, 505 U.S. 833, 895 (1992).

[11]   *Ohio v. Akron Center for Reproductive Health*, 497 U.S. 502 (1990); *Rust v. Sullivan*, 500 U.S. 173 (1991).

[12]   Brief for Respondents at 23-24, *Ayotte v. Planned Parenthood of Northern New England* (No. 04-1144).

[13]   *See Women's Med. Prof. Corp. v. Voinovich*, 130 F.3d 187 (6th Cir. 1997), *cert. denied*, 523 U.S. 1036 (1998); *Jane L. v. Bangerter*, 102 F.3d 1112 (10th Cir. 1996), *cert. denied sub nom., Leavitt v. Jane L.*, 520 U.S. 1274 (1997); *Planned Parenthood, Sioux Falls Clinic v. Miller*, 63 F.3d 1452 (8th Cir. 1995), *cert. denied sub nom., Janklow v. Planned Parenthood*, 517 U.S.

1174 (1996); *A Woman's Choice – East Side Women's Clinic v. Newman*, 305 F.3d 684 (7th Cir. 2002), *cert. denied*, 537 U.S. 1192 (2003).

[14] *See* Center for Reproductive Rights, *Restrictions on Young Women's Access to Abortion Services*, *at* [http://www.crlp.org/pub_fac_restrictions.html].

In: Family Structure and Support Issues
Editor: A. E. Bennett, pp. 111-134
ISBN: 1-60021-340-5
© 2007 Nova Science Publishers, Inc.

Chapter 9

SAME-SEX MARRIAGES: LEGAL ISSUES[*]

Alison M. Smith

ABSTRACT

Massachusetts became the first state to legalize marriage between same-sex couples on May 17, 2004, as a result of a November 2003 decision by the state's highest court that denying gay and lesbian couples the right to marry violated the state's constitution. Currently, federal law does not recognize same-sex marriages. This chapter discusses the Defense of Marriage Act (DOMA), P.L. 104-199, which prohibits federal recognition of same-sex marriages and allows individual states to refuse to recognize such marriages performed in other states, and discusses the potential legal challenges to DOMA. Moreover, this chapter summarizes the legal principles applied in determining the validity of a marriage contracted in another state, surveys the various approaches employed by states to prevent same-sex marriage, and examines the recent House and Senate Resolutions introduced in the 109th Congress proposing a constitutional amendment (H.J.Res. 39, S.J.Res. 1, and S.J.Res. 13) and limiting Federal courts' jurisdiction to hear or determine any question pertaining to the interpretation of DOMA (H.R. 1100).

Massachusetts became the first state to legalize marriage between same-sex couples on May 17, 2004, as a result of a November 2003 decision by the state's highest court that denying gay and lesbian couples the right to marry violated the

---

[*] Excerpted from CRS Report RL31994, dated December 5, 2005.

state's constitution.[1] Currently neither federal law nor any state law affirmatively allows gay or lesbian couples to marry. On the federal level, Congress enacted the Defense of Marriage Act (DOMA) to prohibit recognition of same-sex marriages for purposes of federal enactments. States, such as Arkansas,[2] Alaska, Georgia,[3] Hawaii, Kansas,[4] Kentucky,[5] Louisiana,[6] Michigan,[7] Mississippi,[8] Missouri,[9] Montana,[10] Nebraska,[11] Nevada, North Dakota,[12] Ohio,[13] Oklahoma,[14] Oregon,[15] Texas,[16] and Utah have enacted state constitutional amendments limiting marriage to one man and one woman. Twenty-six other states have enacted statutes limiting marriage in some manner.[17] Table 1 summarizes these various approaches.

DEFENSE OF MARRIAGE ACT (DOMA)[18]

In 1996, Congress enacted the DOMA "[t]o define and protect the institution of marriage." It allows all states, territories, possessions, and Indian tribes to refuse to recognize an act of any other jurisdiction that designates a relationship between individuals of the same sex as a marriage. In part, DOMA states:

> No State, territory, or possession of the United States, or Indian tribe, shall be required to give effect to any public act, record, or judicial proceeding of any other State, territory, possession, or tribe respecting a relationship between persons of the same sex that is treated as a marriage under the laws of such other State, territory, possession, or tribe, or a right or claim arising from such relationship.[19]

Furthermore, DOMA goes on to declare that the terms "marriage" and "spouse," as used in federal enactments, exclude homosexual marriage.

> In determining the meaning of any Act of Congress, or of any ruling, regulation, or interpretation of the various administrative bureaus and agencies of the United States, the word 'marriage' means only a legal union between one man and one woman as husband and wife, and the word 'spouse' refers only to a person of the opposite sex who is a husband or a wife.[20]

POTENTIAL CONSTITUTIONAL CHALLENGES TO DOMA[21]

Full Faith and Credit Clause

Some argue that DOMA is an unconstitutional exercise of Congress' authority under the full faith and credit clause of the U.S. Constitution.[22] Article IV, section 1 of the Constitution, the Full Faith and Credit Clause states:

> Full Faith and Credit shall be given in each State to the public Acts, Records, and judicial Proceedings of every other State; And the Congress may by general Laws prescribe the Manner in which such Acts, Records and Proceedings shall be proved, and the Effect thereof.

Opponents argue that, while Congress has authority to pass laws that enable acts, judgments and the like to be given effect in other States, it has no constitutional power to pass a law permitting States to deny full faith and credit to another State's laws and judgments.[23] Conversely, some argue that DOMA does nothing more than simply restate the power granted to the States by the full faith and credit clause.[24] While there is no judicial precedent on this issue, it would appear that Congress' general authority to "prescribe...the effect" of public acts arguably gives it discretion to define the "effect" so that a particular public act is not due full faith and credit. It would appear that the plain reading of the clause would encompass both expansion and contraction.[25]

Equal Protection

Congress' authority to legislate in this manner under the full faith and credit clause, if the analysis set out above is accepted, does not conclude the matter. There are constitutional constraints upon federal legislation. One that is relevant is the equal protection clause and the effect of the Supreme Court's decision in *Romer v. Evans*,[26] which struck down under the equal protection clause a referendum-adopted provision of the Colorado Constitution, which repealed local ordinances that provided civil-rights protections for gay persons and which prohibited all governmental action designed to protect homosexuals from discrimination. The Court held that, under the equal protection clause, legislation adverse to homosexuals was to be scrutinized under a "rational basis" standard of review.[27] The classification failed to pass even this deferential standard of review, because it imposed a special disability on homosexuals not visited on any other class of people and it could not be justified by any of the arguments made by the State. The State argued that its purpose for the amendment was two-fold: (1) to respect the freedom of association rights of other citizens, such as landlords and employers) who objected to homosexuality; and (2) to serve the state's interest in conserving resources to fight discrimination against other protected groups.

DOMA can be distinguished from the Colorado amendment. DOMA's legislative history indicates that it was intended to protect federalism interests and state sovereignty in the area of domestic relations, historically a subject of almost exclusive state concern. Moreover, it permits but does not require States to deny recognition to same-sex marriages in other States, affording States with strong public policy concerns the discretion to effectuate that policy. Thus, it can be argued that DOMA is grounded not in hostility to homosexuals but in an intent to afford the States the discretion to act as their public policy on same-sex marriage dictates.

Substantive Due Process (Right to Privacy)

Another possibly applicable constitutional constraint is the Due Process Clause of the Fourteenth Amendment and the effect of the Supreme Court's decision in *Lawrence v. Texas*,[28] which struck down under the due process clause a state statute criminalizing certain private sexual acts between homosexuals. The Court held that the Fourteenth Amendment's due process privacy guarantee extends to protect consensual sex between adult homosexuals. The Court noted that the Due Process right to privacy protects certain personal decisions from governmental interference. These personal decisions include issues regarding contraceptives, abortion, marriage, procreation, and family relations.[29] The Court extended this right to privacy to cover adult consensual homosexual sodomy.

It is currently unclear what impact, if any, the Court's decision in *Lawrence* will have on legal challenges to laws prohibiting same-sex marriage. On the one hand, this decision can be viewed as affirming a broad constitutional right to sexual privacy. Conversely, the Court distinguished this case from cases involving minors and "whether the government must give formal recognition to any relationship that homosexual persons seek to enter."[30] Courts may seek to distinguish statutes prohibiting same-sex marriage from statutes criminalizing homosexual conduct. Courts may view the preservation of the institution of marriage as sufficient justification for statutes banning same-sex marriage.

Moreover, courts may view the public recognition of marriage differently than the sexual conduct of homosexuals in the privacy of their own homes.

INTERSTATE RECOGNITION OF MARRIAGE

DOMA opponents take the position that the Full Faith and Credit Clause would obligate States to recognize same-sex marriages contracted in States in which they are authorized. This conclusion is far from evident as this clause applies principally to the interstate recognition and enforcement of judgments.[31] It is settled law that final judgments are entitled to full faith and credit, regardless of other states' public policies, provided the issuing state had jurisdiction over the parties and the subject matter.[32] The Full Faith and Credit Clause has rarely been used by courts to validate marriages because marriages are not "legal judgments."

As such, questions concerning the validity of an out-of-state marriage are generally resolved without reference to the Full Faith and Credit Clause. In the legal sense, marriage is a "civil contract" created by the States which establishes certain duties and confers certain benefits.[33] Validly entering the contract creates the marital status; the duties and benefits attached by a State are incidents of that status. As such, the general tendency, based on comity rather than on compulsion under the Full Faith and Credit Clause, is to recognize marriages contracted in other States even if they could not have been celebrated in the recognizing State.

The general rule of validation for marriage is to look to the law of the place where the marriage was celebrated. A marriage satisfying the contracting State's requirements will usually be held valid everywhere.[34] Many States provide by statute that a marriage that is valid where contracted is valid within the State. This "place of celebration" rule is then subject to a number of exceptions, most of which are narrowly construed. The most common exception to the "place of celebration" rule is for marriages deemed contrary to the forum's strong public policy. Several States, such as Connecticut,[35] Idaho,[36] Illinois,[37] Kansas,[38] Missouri,[39] Pennsylvania,[40] South Carolina,[41] and Tennessee[42] provide an exception to this general rule by declaring out-of-state marriages void if against the State's public policy or if entered into with the intent to evade the law of the State. This exception applies only where another State's law violates "some fundamental principle of justice, some prevalent conception of good morals, some deep-rooted tradition of the common weal."[43]

Section 283 of the Restatement (Second) of Law provides:

1. The validity of marriage will be determined by the local law of the state which, with respect to the particular issue, has the most significant relationship to the spouses and the marriage under the principles stated in § 6.
2. A marriage which satisfies the requirements of the state where the marriage was contracted will everywhere be recognized as valid unless it violates the strong public policy of another state which had the most significant relationship to the spouses and the marriage at the time of the marriage.

STATES' RESPONSES

State Litigation

Massachusetts, unlike twenty-six States and the federal government, has not adopted a "defense of marriage statute" defining marriage as a union between a man and woman.[44] On April 11, 2001, a Boston-based, homosexual rights group, Gay Lesbian Advocates and Defenders (GLAD) filed suit against the Massachusetts Department of Public Health on behalf of seven same-sex couples. The plaintiffs claimed that "refusing same-sex couples the opportunity to apply for a marriage license" violates Massachusetts' law and various portions of the Massachusetts Constitution. GLAD's brief argued the existence of a fundamental right to marry "the person of one's choosing" in the due process provisions of the Massachusetts Constitution and asserted that the marriage laws, which allow both men and women to marry, violate equal protection provisions.[45]

The Superior Court rejected the plaintiffs' arguments after exploring the application of the word marriage, the construction of marriage statutes and finally, the historical purpose of marriage. The trial court found that based on history and the actions of the people's elected representatives, a right to same-sex marriage was not so rooted in tradition that a failure to recognize it violated fundamental liberty, nor was it implicit in ordered liberty.[46] Moreover, the court held that in excluding same-sex couples from marriage, the Commonwealth did not deprive them of substantive due process, liberty, or freedom of speech or association.[47] The court went on to find that limiting marriage to opposite-sex couples was rationally related to a legitimate state interest in encouraging procreation.[48]

On November 18, 2003, the Massachusetts Supreme Judicial Court overruled the lower court and held that under the Massachusetts Constitution, the Commonwealth could not deny the protections, benefits, and obligations attendant on marriage to two individuals of the same sex who wish to marry.[49] The court concluded that interpreting the statutory term "marriage" to apply only to male-female unions, lacked a rational basis for either due process or equal protection purposes under the state's constitution. Moreover, the court found that such a limitation was not justified by the state's interest in providing a favorable setting for procreation and had no rational relationship to the state's interests in ensuring that children be raised in optimal settings and in conservation of state and private financial resources.[50] The court reasoned that the laws of civil marriage did not privilege procreative heterosexual intercourse, nor contain any requirement that applicants for marriage licenses attest to their ability or intention to conceive children by coitus. Moreover, the court reasoned that the state has no power to provide varying levels of protection to children based on the circumstances of birth. As for the state's interest in conserving scarce state and private financial resources, the court found that the state failed to produce any evidence to support its assertion that same-sex couples were less financially interdependent than opposite-sex couples. In addition, Massachusetts marriage laws do not condition receipt of public and private financial benefits to married individuals on a demonstration of financial dependence on each other.[51] As this decision is based on the Commonwealth's constitution, it is not reviewable by the U.S. Supreme Court. The court stayed its decision for 180 days to give the Legislature time to enact legislation "as it may deem appropriate in light of this opinion."[52]

On February 3, 2004, the court ruled, in an advisory opinion to the state senate, that civil unions are not the constitutional equivalent of civil marriage.[53] The court reasoned that the establishment of civil unions for same-sex couples would create a separate class of citizens by status discrimination which would violate the equal protection and due process requirements of the Constitution of the Commonwealth.[54]

While the aforementioned opinions deal exclusively with a state constitution,[55] an Arizona Court of Appeals exercising its discretion to accept jurisdiction based on the issue of first impression, held that the fundamental right to marry protected by the Fourteenth Amendment as well as the Arizona Constitution did not encompass the right to marry a same-sex partner.[56] Moreover, the court found that the state had a legitimate interest in encouraging procreation and child rearing within the marital relationship and limiting that relationship to opposite-sex couples.

In light of the Supreme Court's recent decision in *Lawrence*, the petitioners argued that the Arizona statute prohibiting same-sex marriages violated their fundamental right to marry and their right to equal protection under the laws, both of which are guaranteed by the federal and state constitutions. The Arizona court rejected the petitioners' argument that the Supreme Court in *Lawrence* implicitly recognized that the fundamental right to marry includes the freedom to choose a same-sex spouse.[57] The court viewed the *Lawrence* language as acknowledging a homosexual person's "right to define his or her own existence, and achieve the type of individual fulfillment that is the hallmark of a free society, by entering a homosexual relationship."[58] However, the court declined to view the language as stating that such a right includes the choice to enter a state-sanctioned, same-sex marriage.[59]

As such, the court reviewed the constitutionality of the challenged statutes using a rational basis analysis and found that the state has a legitimate interest in encouraging procreation and child-rearing within the marital relationship, and that limiting marriage to opposite-sex couples is rationally related to that interest. Moreover, the court said that while the state's reasoning is debatable, it is not arbitrary or irrational. Consequently, the court upheld the challenged statutes.

STATE CONSTITUTIONAL AMENDMENTS

Arkansas

Marriage consists only of the union of one man and one woman. Legal status for unmarried persons which is identical or substantially similar to marital status shall not be valid or recognized in Arkansas, except that the Legislature may recognize a common law marriage from another state between a man and a woman. The Legislature has the power to determine the capacity of persons to marry, subject to this amendment, and the legal rights, obligations, privileges and immunities of marriage.[60]

Georgia

This state shall recognize as marriage only the union of man and woman. Marriages between persons of the same sex are prohibited in this state. No union between persons of the same sex shall be recognized by this state as entitled to the benefits of marriage. This state shall not give effect to any public act, record or judicial proceeding of any other state or jurisdiction respecting a relationship between persons of the same sex that is treated as a marriage under the laws of such other state or jurisdiction. The courts of this state shall have no jurisdiction to grant a divorce or separate maintenance with respect to any such relationship or otherwise to consider or rule on any of the parties' respective rights arising as a result of or in connection with such relationship.[61]

Kansas

The marriage contract is to be considered in law as a civil contract. Marriage shall be constituted by one man and one woman only. All other marriages are declared to be contrary to the public policy of this state and are void.

No relationship, other than a marriage, shall be recognized by the state as entitling the parties to the rights or incidents of marriage.[62]

Kentucky

Only a marriage between one man and one woman shall be valid or recognized as a marriage in Kentucky. A legal status identical or substantially similar to that of marriage for unmarried individuals shall not be valid or recognized.[63]

Louisiana

Marriage in the state of Louisiana shall consist only of the union of one man and one woman. No official or court of the state of Louisiana shall construe this constitution or any state law to require that marriage or the legal incidents thereof be conferred upon any member of a union other than the union of one man and one woman. A legal status identical or substantially similar to that of marriage for unmarried individuals shall not be valid or recognized. No official or court of the state of Louisiana shall recognize any marriage contracted in any other jurisdiction which is not the union of one man and one woman to the state constitution.[64]

Michigan

To secure and preserve the benefits of marriage for our society and for future generations of children, the union of one man and one woman in marriage shall be the only agreement recognized as a marriage or similar union for any purpose.[65]

Missouri

That to be valid and recognized in this state, a marriage shall exist only between a man and a woman.[66]

Montana

Only a marriage between one man and one woman shall be valid or recognized as a marriage in this state.

Mississippi

Marriage may take place and may be valid under the laws of this state only between a man and a woman. A marriage in another state or foreign jurisdiction between persons of the same gender, regardless of when the marriage took place, may not be recognized in this state and is void and unenforceable under the laws of this state.[67]

North Dakota

Marriage consists only of the legal union between a man and a woman. No other domestic union, however denominated, may be recognized as a marriage or given the same or substantially equivalent effect.

Ohio

Only a union between one man and one woman may be a marriage valid in or recognized by this state and its political subdivisions. This state and its political subdivisions shall not create or recognize a legal status for relationships of unmarried individuals that intends to approximate the design, qualities, significance or effect of marriage.

Oklahoma

Marriage in this state shall consist only of the union of one man and one woman. Neither this constitution nor any other provision of law shall be construed to require that marital status or the legal incidents thereof be conferred upon unmarried couples or groups. A marriage between persons of the same gender performed in another state shall not be recognized as valid and binding in this state as of the date of the marriage. Any person knowingly issuing a marriage license in violation of this section shall be guilty of a misdemeanor.[68]

Oregon

It is the policy of Oregon, and its political subdivisions, that only a marriage between one man and one woman shall be valid or legally recognized as a marriage.[69]

Texas

Marriage in this state shall consist only of the union of one man and one woman. This state or a political subdivision of this state may not create or recognize any legal status identical or similar to marriage.[70]

Utah

Marriage consists only of the legal union between a man and a woman. No other domestic status or union, however denominated, between persons is valid or recognized or may be authorized, sanctioned or given the same or substantially equivalent legal effect as a marriage.[71]

State *"Civil Union" Laws*

Civil union/domestic partnership laws confer certain rights and benefits upon domestic partners which vary depending on state law. Some of these rights and benefits include laws relating to title, tenure, descent and distribution, intestate succession; causes of action related to or dependent upon spousal status,[72] including an action for wrongful death,[73] emotional distress, or loss of consortium; probate law and procedure; adoption law and procedure; insurance benefits; workers' compensation rights; laws relating to medical care and treatment, hospital visitation and notification; family leave benefits; public assistance benefits under state laws and laws relating to state taxes.[74]

For example, in Vermont, civil union status is available to two persons of the same sex who are unrelated[75] and affords parties "the same benefits, protections and responsibilities under Vermont law, whether they derive from statute, policy, administrative or court rule, common law or any other source of civil law, as are granted to spouses in a marriage."[76] Domestic partnership laws in California,[77] Hawaii,[78] and New Jersey[79] also offer some marital benefits to same-sex couples, although not as comprehensive as Vermont's or Connecticut's civil unions.[80]

PENDING FEDERAL LEGISLATION

Several bills have been introduced in the 109th Congress to address the issue of same-sex marriage.[81] For example, on January 24, 2005, S.J.Res. 1, a proposed constitutional amendment was introduced. The text of the proposed constitutional amendment is as follows:

> Marriage in the United States shall consist only of the union of a man and a woman. Neither this Constitution, nor the constitution of any State, shall be construed to require that marriage or the legal incidents thereof be conferred upon any union other than the union of a man and a woman.

Similar proposed constitutional amendments include S.J.Res. 13, introduced on April 14, 2005,[82] and H.J.Res. 39, introduced on March 17, 2005.[83] In addition, H.R. 1100, introduced on March 3, 2005, would amend title 28 of the United State Code to limit Federal court jurisdiction over questions under DOMA.[84]

Table 1. State Statutes Defining "Marriage"

State	Statute	Marriage definition[a]	Non-Recognition
Alabama	ALA. CODE § 30-1-19 (2003)	X	X
Alaska	ALASKA STAT. § 25.05.011 (2003)	X	
Arizona	ARIZ. REV. STAT. § 25-101 (2003)		X
Arkansas	ARK. CODE ANN. § 9-11-109 (2003)	X	
California	CAL. FAM. CODE § 300 (2003)	X	
Colorado	COLO. REV. STAT. § 14-2-104 (2003)	X	
Connecticut	Judicial Interpretation		X[b]
Delaware	DEL. CODE ANN. tit.13 § 101 (2002)		X
Florida	FLA. STAT. Ch. 741.04 (2002)	X	
Georgia	GA. CODE ANN. § 19-3-3.1 (2002)		X
Hawaii	HAW. REV. STAT. ANN. § 572-1 (2003)	X	
Idaho*	IDAHO CODE § 32-209 (2003)	X	
Illinois*	750 ILL. COMP. STAT. 5/201 (2003)	X	X
Indiana	IND. CODE ANN. § 31-11-1-1 (2003)	X	X
Iowa	IOWA CODE § 595.2 (2003)	X	
Kansas*	KAN. STAT. ANN. § 23-101 (2002)	X	
Kentucky	KY. REV. STAT. ANN. § 402.020 (2002)		X
Louisiana	LA. CIV. CODE art. 86 (2003)	X	
Maine	ME. REV. STAT. ANN. tit. 19, § 701 (2003)		X
Maryland	MD. CODE ANN. FAM. LAW § 2- 201 (2002)	X	
Massachusetts	Judicial Interpretation	X[c]	
Michigan	MICH. COMP. LAWS § 551.1 (2003)	X	X
Minnesota	MINN. STAT. § 517.01 (2002)	X	
Mississippi	MISS. CODE ANN. § 93-1-1 (2003)		X
Missouri*	MO. REV. STAT. § 451.022 (2003)		X
Montana	MONT. CODE ANN. § 40-1-103 (2002)	X	
Nebraska	NEB. REV. STAT. ANN. art. 1, § 29 (2002)		X
Nevada	NEV. REV. STAT. ANN. §122.020 (2003)	X	
New Hampshire	N.H. REV. STAT. ANN. § 457:2 (2002)		X
New Jersey	Judicial Interpretation	X[d]	
New Mexico	N.M. STAT. ANN § 40-1-1 (2002)	X[e]	
New York	Judicial Interpretation	X[f]	
North Carolina	N.C. GEN. STAT. § 51-1.2 (2003)		X

Table 1. Continued

State	Statute	Marriage definition[a]	Non-Recognition
North Dakota	N.D. CENT. CODE § 14-03-01 (2002)	X	
Ohio*	OHIO REV. CODE ANN. §3101	X[g]	X
Oklahoma	OKLA. STAT. tit. 43 § 3.1 (2003)		X
Oregon	OR. REV. STAT. § 106.010 (2001)	X[h]	
Pennsylvania*	PA. STAT. ANN. tit. 23 § 1704 (2002)		X
Rhode Island	R.I. GEN. LAWS § 15-1-1 (2002)	X[i]	
South Carolina*	S.C. CODE ANN. § 20-1-10 (2002)		X
South Dakota	S. D. CODIFIED LAWS § 25-1-1 (2002)	X	
Tennessee*	TENN. CODE. ANN. § 36-3-113 (2003)	X	
Texas	TEX. FAM. CODE ANN. § 2.001 (2002)	X	
Utah	UTAH CODE ANN. § 30-1-2 (2003)		X
Vermont	VT. STAT. ANN. tit. 15 § 8 (2003)	X	
Virginia	VA. CODE ANN. § 20-45.2 (2003)		X
Washington	WASH. REV. CODE ANN. § 26.04.010 (2003)	X	
West Virginia	W. VA. CODE § 48-2-603 (2003)		X
Wisconsin	WIS. STAT. § 765.01 (2002)	X[j]	
Wyoming	WYO. STAT. § 20-1-101 (2003)	X	
Puerto Rico	P.R. LAWS ANN. tit. 31, § 221 (2002)	X	

Note: States marked with an asterisk have a statute establishing same-sex unions as violation of the state's public policy.

[a] Marriage consists of a contract between one man and one woman.

[b] Since nothing in the statute, legislative history, court rules, case law, or public policy permitted same-sex marriage or recognized the parties' Vermont civil union as a marriage, the trial court lacked jurisdiction to dissolve the union.

[c] The Supreme Judicial Court has interpreted "marriage," within Massachusetts' statutes, "as the union of one man and one woman." *Adoption of Tammy*, 619 N.E.2d 315 (1993). However, in *Goodridge v. Dept. of Public Health*, 798 N.E.2d 941 (Mass. 2003), the court construed the term "marriage" to mean the voluntary union of two persons as spouses, to the exclusion of all others.

[d] Although no specific language in this statute or other New Jersey marriage statutes prohibits same-sex marriages, the meaning of marriage as a heterosexual institution was so firmly established that the court could not disregard its plain meaning and the clear intent of the legislature. *Rutgers Council v. Rutgers State University*, 689 A.2d 828 (1997).

[e] Marriage is a civil contract requiring consent of parties.

[f] Marriage has been traditionally defined as the voluntary union of one man and one woman as husband and wife. See e.g., *Fisher v. Fisher*, 250 N.Y. 313, 165 N. E.

460 (1929). A basic assumption, therefore, is that one of the two parties to the union must be male and the other must be female. On the basis of this assumption, the New York courts have consistently viewed it essential to the formation of a marriage that the parties be of opposite sexes.

ᵍ. Effective May 7, 2004.

ʰ· Marriage is a civil contract entered into in person by males at least 17 years of age and females at least 17 years of age, who are otherwise capable, and solemnized in accordance with ORS 106.1

ⁱ Men are forbidden to marry kindred.

ʲ Marriage, so far as its validity at law is concerned, is a civil contract, to which the consent of the parties capable in law of contracting is essential, and which creates the legal status of husband and wife.

Although uniformity may be achieved upon ratification of the proposed constitutional amendments, States would no longer have the flexibility of defining marriage within their borders. Moreover, States may be prohibited from recognizing a same-sex marriage performed and recognized outside of the United States.[85] It appears that this amendment would not impact a State's ability to define civil unions or domestic partnerships and the benefits conferred upon such.

However, an issue may arise regarding the time in which an individual is considered a man or a woman. As the first official document to indicate a person's sex, the designation on the birth certificate "usually controls the sex designation on all later documents."[86] Some courts have held that sexual identity for purposes of marriage is determined by the sex stated on the birth certificate, regardless of subsequent sexual reassignment.[87] However, some argue that this method is flawed, as an infant's sex may be misidentified at birth and the individual may subsequently identify with and conform his or her biology to another sex upon adulthood.[88]

CONCLUSION

States currently possess the authority to decide whether to recognize an out-of-state marriage. The Full Faith and Credit Clause has rarely been used by States to validate marriages because marriages are not "legal judgments." With respect to cases decided under the Full Faith and Credit Clause that involve conflicting State statutes, the Supreme Court generally examines the significant aggregation of contacts the forum has with the parties and the occurrence or transaction to decide which State's law to apply. Similarly, based upon generally accepted legal principles, States routinely decide whether a marriage validly contracted in another jurisdiction will be recognized in-State by examining whether it has a significant relationship with the spouses and the marriage.

Congress is empowered under the Full Faith and Credit Clause of the Constitution to prescribe the manner that public acts, commonly understood to mean legislative acts, records, and proceedings shall be proved and the effect of such acts, records, and proceedings in other States.[89]

The Supreme Court's decisions in *Romer v. Colorado* and *Lawrence v. Texas* may present different issues concerning DOMA's constitutionality. Basically *Romer* appears to stand for the proposition that legislation targeting gays and lesbians is constitutionally impermissible under the Equal Protection Clause unless the legislative classification bears a rational relationship to a legitimate State purpose. Because same-sex marriages are singled out for differential treatment, DOMA appears to create a legislative classification for equal protection purposes that must meet a rational basis test. It is possible that DOMA would survive constitutional scrutiny under *Romer* inasmuch as the statute was enacted to protect the traditional institution of marriage. Moreover, DOMA does not prohibit States from recognizing same-sex marriage if they so choose.

Lawrence appears to stand for the proposition that the zone of privacy protected by the Due Process Clause of the Fourteen Amendment extends to adult, consensual sex between homosexuals. *Lawrence's* implication for statutes banning same-sex marriages and the constitutional validity of the DOMA are unclear.

REFERENCES

[1] Goodridge v. Dept. of Public Health, 798 N.E.2d 941 (Mass. 2003).

[2] Voters approved the constitutional ban on November 2, 2004.

[3] Voters approved the constitutional ban on November 2, 2004.

[4] Voters approved the constitutional ban on April 5, 2005.

[5] Voters approved the constitutional ban on November 2, 2004.

[6] Voters approved the constitutional ban on September 18, 2004. The Louisiana Supreme Court reversed a state district judge's ruling striking down the amendment on the grounds that it violated a provision of the state constitution requiring that an amendment cover only one subject. The Court found that each provision of the amendment is germane to the single object of defense of marriage and constitutes an element of the plan advanced to achieve this object. Forum for Equality PAC v. McKeithen, 893 So.3d 715

(La. 2005). Three other states that also have single-subject requirements, Georgia, Ohio and Oklahoma, may face legal challenges similar to the one in Louisiana.

[7] Voters approved the constitutional ban on November 2, 2004.

[8] Voters approved the constitutional ban on November 2, 2004.

[9] Voters approved the constitutional ban on August 3, 2004.

[10] Voters approved the constitutional ban on November 2, 2004.

[11] A U.S. district court judge struck down Nebraska's ban on gay marriage, saying that the ban "imposes significant burdens on both the expressive and intimate associational rights" of gays "and creates a significant barrier to the plaintiffs' right to petition or to participate in the political process." Citizens for Equal Protection Inc., v. Bruning, 368 F.Supp.2d 980 (D. NE May 12, 2005).

[12] Voters approved the constitutional ban on November 2, 2004.

[13] Voters approved the constitutional ban on November 2, 2004.

[14] Voters approved the constitutional ban on November 2, 2004.

[15] Voters approved the constitutional ban on November 2, 2004. On April 4, 2005, the Oregon Supreme Court invalidated Multnomah County same-sex marriages, stating that the marriage licenses were issued to same-sex couples without authority and were void at the time they were issued. Li v. State, 110 P.3d 91 (Or. 2005).

[16] Voters approved the constitutional ban on November 8, 2005.

[17] These states are: Alabama, Arizona, California, Colorado, Delaware, Florida, Idaho, Illinois, Indiana, Iowa, Kansas, Maine, Maryland, Minnesota, New Hampshire, North Carolina, Pennsylvania, South Carolina, South Dakota, Tennessee, Texas, Vermont, Virginia, Washington, West Virginia, and Wyoming.

[18] P.L. 104-199, 110 Stat. 2419 (codified at 1 U.S.C. § 7 and 28 U.S.C. § 1738C).

[19] 28 U.S.C. §1738C.

[20] 1 U.S.C. § 7.

[21] It should be noted that a federal bankruptcy court in the Western District of Washington found DOMA constitutional. Two American women, married in British Columbia, Canada filed a joint bankruptcy petition in Tacoma, challenging the definitional part of DOMA. The court ruled that there was no fundamental constitutional right to marry someone of the same sex and that DOMA did not violate the Fourth, Fifth or Tenth amendments, nor the principles of comity. In re Lee Kandu and Ann C. Kandu, No. 03-51312 (Western District of Washington, Aug. 17, 2004). This decision is not

binding on other courts. In Wilson v. Ake, a same-sex couple sought a declaration that their marriage was valid for federal and Florida law purposes. To issue such a declaration, the court would have had to invalidate both the Federal DOMA and the Florida statutes defining marriage the same way and expressly forbidding courts to recognize same-sex marriages from other states. The Wilson court declined to invalidate any of the relevant statutes finding that (1) DOMA did not violate the Full Faith and Credit Clause; (2) the right to marry a person of the same sex was not a fundamental right guaranteed by the Due Process Clause; (3) homosexuals were not a suspect class warranting strict scrutiny of equal protection claim; (4) under a rational basis analysis, DOMA did not violate equal protection or due process guarantees; and (5) the Florida statute prohibiting same-sex marriage is constitutional. Wilson v. Ake, 354 F.Supp.3d 1298 (M.D. Florida, Jan. 19, 2005). Moreover, the Wilson court found that it was bound by the U.S. Supreme Court's decision in Baker v. Nelson, 191 N.W.2d 185 (1971), appeal dismissed, 409 U.S. 810 (1972). In Baker v. Nelson, two adult males' application for a marriage license was denied by the County clerk because the petitioners were of the same sex. The plaintiffs appealed to the Minnesota Supreme Court. Plaintiffs argued that Minnesota Statute § 517.08, which did not authorize marriage between persons of the same sex, violated the First, Eighth, Ninth and Fourteenth Amendments of the U.S. Constitution. The Minnesota Supreme Court rejected plaintiffs' assertion that "the right to marry without regard to the sex of the parties is a fundamental right of all persons" and held that § 517.08 did not violate the Due Process Clause or Equal Protection Clause. 191 N.W.2d at 186-87. The plaintiffs then appealed the Minnesota Supreme Court's ruling to the U.S. Supreme Court pursuant to 28 U.S.C. § 1257(2). Under 28 U.S.C. § 1257, the Supreme Court had no discretion to refuse to adjudicate the case on its merits. The Supreme Court ultimately dismissed the appeal "for want of a substantial federal question." Baker, 408 U.S. at 810. The Wilson court, relying on Hicks v. Miranda (422 U.S. 332 (1975)), found that a dismissal for lack of a substantial federal question constitutes an adjudication on the merits that is binding on lower federal courts.

[22] U.S. Const. art. IV, § 1.

[23] See 142 Cong. Rec. S5931-33 (June 6, 1996) (statement introducing Professor Laurence H. Tribe's letter into the record concluding that DOMA "would be an unconstitutional attempt by Congress to limit the full faith and credit clause of the Constitution.").

[24] See Paige E. Chabora, Congress' Power Under the Full Faith and Credit Clause and the Defense of Marriage Act of 1996, 76 Neb. L. Rev. 604, 621-35 (1997).

[25] See e.g., Wilson v. Ake, 354 F.Supp.2d at 1302 (finding that DOMA was an appropriate exercise of Congress' power to regulate conflicts between the laws of different States, and holding otherwise would create "a license for a single State to create national policy.").

[26] 517 U.S. 620 (1996).

[27] Id.

[28] 539 U.S. 558 (2003). For a legal analysis of this decision, refer to CRS Report RL31681, Homosexuality and the Constitution: A Legal Analysis of the Supreme Court Ruling in Lawrence v. Texas by Jody Feder.

[29] Lawrence v. Texas, 539 U.S. 558 (2003).

[30] Id. at 2484. See e.g., Wilson v. Ake, 354 F.Supp.2d at 1306 (declining to interpret Lawrence as creating a fundamental right to same-sex marriage).

[31] See H.Rept. 104-664, 1996 U.S.C.C.A.N. 2905 (stating that "marriage licensure is not a judgment."). See also, 28 U.S.C. § 1738 (defining which acts, records and judicial proceeding are afforded full faith and credit).

[32] Restatement (Second) of Conflict of Laws § 107.

[33] On the state level, common examples of nonnegotiable marital rights and obligations include distinct income tax filing status; public assistance such as health and welfare benefits; default rules concerning community property distribution and control; dower, curtesy and inheritance rights; child custody, child agreements; name change rights; spouse and marital communications privileges in legal proceedings; and the right to bring wrongful death, and certain other, legal actions.

[34] See 2 Restatement (Second) of Conflict of Laws § 283.

[35] Conn. Gen Stat. Ann. § 45a-803-4.

[36] Idaho Code § 32-209.

[37] 750 Ill. Comp. Stat. 5/201.

[38] Kan. Stat. Ann. § 23-101.

[39] Mo. Rev. Stat. § 451.022.

[40] Pa. Stat. Ann. tit. 23 § 1704.

[41] S.C. Code Ann. § 20-1-10.

[42] Tenn. Code Ann. § 36-3-113.

[43] Loucks v. Standard Oil Co., 120 N.E. 198, 202 (N.Y. 1918)(defining public policy as a valid reason for closing the forum to suit); see e.g. Shea v. Shea, 63 N.E.2d 113 (N.Y. 1945)(finding that a common law marriage validly

contracted in another state should not be recognized as common law marriage in New York as it was prohibited by statute).

[44] It should be noted that, prior to the Goodridge case, in Adoption of Tammy, 619 N.E. 2d 315 (Mass. 1993), the Supreme Judicial Court had interpreted "marriage" to mean "the union of one man and one woman."

[45] Hilary Goodridge v. Dept. of Public Health, No. 01-1647-A, 2002 Mass. Super LEXIS 153 (Suffolk County, Super. Ct. May 7, 2002).

[46] Id.

[47] Id.

[48] Id.

[49] Hillary Goodridge v. Dept. of Public Health, 798 N.E.2d 941 (Mass. 2003).

[50] Id. at *14 (stating that it "cannot be rational under our laws, and indeed is not permitted, to penalize children by depriving them of state benefits because the state disapproves of their parents' sexual orientation.")

[51] Id. at 15.

[52] Id. at *18.

[53] The state Senate asked the court whether it would be sufficient for the legislature to pass a law allowing same-sex civil unions that would confer "all of the benefits, protections, rights and responsibilities of marriage."

[54] Opinions of the Justices to the Senate, SJC-01963, 802 N.E.2d 565 (Mass. 2004).

[55] There are approximately 20 lawsuits filed which seek same-sex marriage rights under state constitutions. These states include California, Connecticut, Florida, Indiana, Maryland, Nebraska, New Jersey, New York, Oregon and Washington. Washington's Supreme Court is expected to hear appeals of two lower court rulings that struck down the state's DOMA (Anderson v. King County, 2004 WK 1738447, Wash. Super, Aug. 4, 2004 and Castle v. State, 20004 WL 1985215, Wash. Super., Sept. 7, 2004). A lawsuit pending in California has been appealed to the state's highest court.

[56] Standhardt v. Superior Court of the State of Arizona, 77 P.3d 451 (Ariz. Ct. App. 2003).

[57] Id. at 457.

[58] Id.

[59] See also, Morrison v. Sadler, 2003 WL 23119998 (Ind. Super. May 7, 2003)(holding that the state's law "promotes the state's interest in encouraging procreation to occur in a context where both biological parents are present to raise the child."); Lewis v. Harris, 2003 WL 23191114 (N.J.Super.L. Nov. 5, 2003)(holding that the right to marry does not include a fundamental right to same-sex marriage).

[60] AR. CONST. Amend. 83, sec. 1.

[61] GA. CONST. Art. I., §IV.

[62] KS CONST. Art. 15, § 16.

[63] KY. CONST. § 233A.

[64] LA. CONST. Art. XII, §15. The Louisiana Supreme Court reversed a state district judge's ruling striking down the amendment on the grounds that it violated a provision of the state constitution requiring that an amendment cover only one subject. The Court found that each provision of the amendment is germane to the single object of defense of marriage and constitutes an element of the plan advanced to achieve this object. Forum for Equality PAC v. McKeithen, 893 So. 2d 715 (La., 2005).

[65] MI. CONST., Art. 1, Sec. 25.

[66] MO. CONST., Art. I, Sect. 33.

[67] MISS. CONST. §263-A.

[68] OKLA. CONST. Art. II, §35.

[69] OR. CONST. Art. XV, §5a.

[70] TX CONST. Art. 1, §32.

[71] UTAH CONST. Art. I, §29.

[72] See Salucco v. Alldredge, 2004 WL 864459 (Superior Ct of Mass., Mar. 29, 2004)(exercising its general equity jurisdiction to dissolve a Vermont civil union).

[73] See Langan v. St. Vincent Hosp., 196 Misc.2d 440 (N.Y. Misc. 2003)(finding that New York's statutes did not prohibit recognition of a same-sex union nor was such a union against New York's public policy on marriage thus recognizing the same-sex partner as a spouse for purposes of New York's wrongful death statute), overruled by Langan v. St. Vincent Hosp., 802 N.Y.S. 2d 476 (NY AD 2 Dept., 2005).

[74] Constitutional amendments approved in Arkansas, Georgia, Kansas, Kentucky, Michigan, North Dakota, Oklahoma, Ohio and Utah contain language which state that a legal status which is substantially similar to marriage (i.e. civil unions or domestic partnerships) may not be recognized.

[75] Vt. Stat. Ann. Tit. 15 §§ 1203, 5163. See also, "The Vermont Guide to Civil Unions" found at

[76] [http://www.sec.state.vt.us/otherprg/civilunions/civilunions.html].

[77] Vt. Stat. Ann. Tit. 15 § 1204. See also, Salucco v. Alldredge, 2004 WL 864459 (Superior Ct of Mass., Mar. 29, 2004)(discussing Vermont's civil union statutes). On October 1, 2005, Connecticut's civil union laws go into effect. A Connecticut civil union will be available to an individual at least 18 years of age, of the same sex as the other party to the civil union, no

more closely related to the other than first cousin and not a party to another civil union or marriage. 2005 Conn. Legis. Serv. P.A. 05-10 (S.S.B. 963).

[78] CA Fam. §§ 297, 298 and 299(extending the rights and duties of marriage to persons registered as domestic partners on and after January 1, 2005). It should be noted that opposite-sex domestic partners over the age of 62 meeting the eligibility requirements of Title II of the Social Security Act (SSA) for old age benefits (as defined in 42 U.S.C. § 402(a)), or Title XVI of the SSA for aged individuals (as defined in 42 U.S.C. § 1381) are eligible to register as domestic partners.

[79] Hawaii's term for domestic partners is "reciprocal beneficiaries." Reciprocal beneficiaries must be eighteen years old, ineligible to marry, and unmarried. This status includes relationships not involving sex or the same residence. Haw. Rev. Stat. § 572C-5; See also, [http://www.hawaii.gov/health/vital-records/reciprocal/index.html] (discussing Hawaii's reciprocal beneficiary status).

[80] The New Jersey Domestic Partnership Act is effective July 11, 2004, and grants legal status to same-sex couples and unmarried, opposite-sex couples age 62 or over under certain New Jersey laws.

[81] Domestic partnerships also exist at the local level. For example, New York City allows residents an opportunity to register their domestic partnerships provided that both individuals are eighteen years of age or older, unmarried or related by blood in a manner that would bar his or her marriage in New York State, have a close and committed personal relationship, live together and have been living together on a continuous basis. N.Y.C. Admin. Code § 3-241. It should be noted that this statute allows both same-sex and opposite-sex partners to register.

[82] Proposed constitutional amendments were introduced in the 108th Congress. H.J.Res. 56 and S.J.Res. 26 text was as follows: Marriage in the United States shall consist only of the union of a man and a woman. Neither this Constitution or the constitution of any State, nor state or federal law, shall be construed to require that marital status or the legal incidents thereof be conferred upon unmarried couples or groups. S.J.Res. 30 was introduced with technical changes to S.J.Res. 26. The text of S.J.Res. 30 and S.J.Res. 40 is as follows: Marriage in the United States shall consist only of the union of a man and a woman. Neither this Constitution, nor the constitution of any State, shall be construed to require that marriage or the legal incidents thereof be conferred upon any union other than the union of a man and a woman. On July 14, 2004, the Senate considered and voted on a

required procedural motion. This motion failed by a vote of 48-50, which prevented further consideration of S.J.Res. 40.

[83] The text of S.J.Res. 13 is as follows: SECTION 1. Marriage in the United States shall consist only of the union of a man and a woman. SECTION 2. Congress shall have the power to enforce this article by appropriate legislation.

[84] The text of H.J.Res. 39 is as follows: SECTION 1. Marriage in the United States shall consist only of a legal union of one man and one woman. SECTION 2. No court of the United States or of any State shall have jurisdiction to determine whether this Constitution or the constitution of any State requires that the legal incidents of marriage be conferred upon any union other than a legal union between one man and one woman. SECTION 3. No State shall be required to give effect to any public act, record, or judicial proceeding of any other State concerning a union between persons of the same sex that is treated as a marriage, or as having the legal incidents of marriage, under the laws of such other State.

[85] H.R. 1100 is identical to H.R. 3313, the Marriage Protection Act of 2003 , introduced during the 108th Congress. On July 22, 2004, the House voted on and passed H.R. 3313. The Senate did not consider the legislation during the 108th Congress.

[86] It appears that the Netherlands, Belgium and Ontario, Canada are the only international jurisdictions that sanction and/or recognize a same-sex union as a "marriage," per se.

[87] Julie A. Greenberg, Defining Male and Female: Intersexuality and the Collision Between Law and Biology, 41 Ariz. L. Rev. 265,309 (1999) (discussing biological characteristics and sexual identity).

[88] See e.g., In re Estate of Gardiner, 42 P.3d 120 (Kan. 2002); Littleton v. Prange, 9 S.W. 3d 223 (Tex. App. 1999); but see, M.T. v. J.T., 355 A.2d 204 (N.J. 1976)(determining an individual's sexual classification for the purpose of marriage encompasses a mental component as well as an anatomical component).

[89] If a mistake was made on the original birth certificate, an amended certificate will sometimes be issued if accompanied by an affidavit from a physician or a court order.

[90] It should be noted that only on five occasions previous to the DOMA has Congress enacted legislation based upon this power. The first, passed in 1790 (1 Stat. 122, codified at 28 U.S.C. § 1738), provides for ways to authenticate acts, records and judicial proceedings. The second, dating from 1804 (2 Stat. 298, codified at 28 U.S.C. 1738), provides methods of

authenticating non-judicial records. Three other Congressional enactments pertain to modifiable family law orders (child custody, 28 U.S.C. § 1738A, child support (28 U.S.C. § 1738B) and domestic protection (18 U.S.C. § 2265)).

INDEX

D

E